contents

AWARDS

Cannes Festival 1994
Palme d'Or

American Academy Awards (Oscars) 1994
Best Original Screenplay

—///—

author of this note Neville Langley is Senior Lecturer in Communication & Creative Arts at Cricklade College, Hampshire, and an Associate Lecturer with the Open University. He is a specialist in Media & Film Studies and has a masters degree from The Winchester School of Art in the History of Modern Art & Design.

YORK FILM NOTES

Pulp Fiction

Director
Quentin Tarantino

Note by Neville Langley

Longman

York Press

York Press
322 Old Brompton Road, London SW5 9JH

Pearson Education Limited
Edinburgh Gate, Harlow, Essex CM20 2JE, United Kingdom
Associated companies, branches and representatives throughout
the world

Stills courtesy of Miramax Films. Screenplay reproduced by kind permission
of Faber & Faber Ltd.

First published 2000

ISBN 0-582-40501-7

Designed by Vicki Pacey
Phototypeset by Gem Graphics, Trenance, Mawgan Porth, Cornwall
Colour reproduction and film output by Spectrum Colour
Printed in Malaysia, KVP

background

trailer

John Travolta. Buster Keaton would have been envious.

Roger Ebert, Chicago Sun-Times

the action in the movie comes under the heading 'Crisis Control'.

Roger Ebert, ibid

Pulp Fiction is a volcanic eruption.

Joan Ellis, Nebbadoon

It's devilishly hard to capture an explosion.

Joan Ellis, ibid

full of wacky juxtapositions.

Joan Ellis, ibid

reading pulp fiction

Pulp Fiction is the redefinition of the gangster/thriller genre, a genre that has been re-worked and re-presented throughout the history of cinema. The cinema audience has always clamoured for stories of the wild side of urban criminal sub-culture, and portrayals of the codes of violence that prevail there.

'*Pulp Fiction* is a volcanic eruption', wrote Joan Ellis in a review from *Nebbadoon*, 'it's devilishly hard to capture an explosion'.

The setting of *Pulp Fiction* is precisely in Los Angeles and metaphorically in any late twentieth century urban American space. It has a stronger sense of location than any actual, landmarked, identifiable place. The film does not try to be a parable of low life in LA. The opening scene is deliberately made strange by not identifying its location; two young

reading pulp fiction background

people, one with an English accent the other accent unclear, in an easily identifiable American diner. Tarantino is not using the convention of an establishing shot, he is pointing out that this is a film that has been made by a film maker. The making of the film is a ritual celebration of the director's passion for movies.

The perception of cities and the evil that they sustain is part of contemporary life. Viewing from a safe distance, in the cinema, representations of civilisation and the barbarity it paradoxically contains is an aspect of the pleasure of living in comfort and security in a hostile and violent environment. *Pulp Fiction* provides a location for the social ritual of celebrating our success in surviving modern life.

Pulp Fiction can be read in a number of different ways. It can be watched purely for the pleasure afforded by a Hollywood mainstream action movie; strong characters and graphic violence combine to make a thrilling spectacle. The dialogue provides a tough foil for the visual effects and action. On what is a relatively well-swept set, the foul language and moody interaction of the chiselled, stereotypical characters evoke the whiff of the streets. The audience is invited into a callous world and given licence to take pleasure in the pain and suffering of those on screen. Alan A. Stone writing in the *Boston Review* in 1994 observed that in 'the scene in which John Travolta's character accidentally blows a young man's brains out most of the audience laughed despite the spatter of blood and brain tissue; and with spontaneous amusement, not the nervous hysteria often heard at horror films', and added that 'Tarantino meant the audience to laugh'.

The film as a spectacular display of physical, verbal and emotional violence is sheer escapism. A means of escape for the audience that goes beyond the boundaries of black humour, where the juxtaposition of violence and comedy is more like a hideously ecstatic collision.

Alan A. Stone commented further that 'The violence of *Pulp Fiction* is essential to its aesthetic' and this suggests another way of reading the film. As an example of art house film making it has a terrible beauty. It deals with loyalty, redemption and love alongside deceit, vengeance and cynical sexuality, all lit in either blinding white sunlight, squalid chiaroscuro or bleeding garish colour. The dialogue is crude and lyrically subtle enough to barely conceal rhyme, rhythm and eloquence.

Another interesting approach is to understand how the characters are portrayed as copies without originals; simulacra. The audience are probably familiar with the actors from previous films made by Tarantino, or more broadly from each individual actor's film career.

Tarantino's reputation in 1994 when *Pulp Fiction* appeared was already well established in Hollywood and around the world. Only just into his thirties he had forced a rapid rise from video store assistant to one of the most in-demand writers and directors in the industry.

director as auteur

It is the case in every mainstream film that the actors bring along with them their own histories, reputations, successes and 'turkeys', their personalities and the images that have developed in the imagination of audiences throughout their careers. This is an inevitable aspect of the process of intertextuality. But in this formula of talent that makes the movie, what is to be said of the presence of the director? This question raises the issue of the director as auteur.

The term is loosely derived from the debate among French film critics in the 1950s and was first coined in the early 1960s by Andrew Sarris to identify the notion that the director is the 'author' of the film. And by claiming authorship of the film, or text, the film can assume the status of a work of art. Just as a piece of literature or a painting has the personality of the author embedded in it, a film too is predominantly the product of the creative inspiration of the director. For example, according to the auteur theory of authorship in film the distinctive quality of the director Jean Renoir is as recognisable in his films as the hand of his father, Auguste Renoir, in his celebrated impressionist paintings. However, the debate about authorship in film is complex and still raging. Some of the more contentious issues raised by the debate are to do with, firstly, collaboration. The making of a film involves a great many people; set designers, camera operators, artistic directors, actors, editors, screen writers and many more.

'I didn't go to film school, I watched movies'.

Is it to be assumed that changing any one or more of these personnel would affect the final cut of the film? Secondly, if the same screenplay were given to two different directors would they produce two free-standing and different works of art? Furthermore, using the analogy of music, how discernible is the hand of the conductor in the concerto played by dozens of musicians making up his orchestra? And so the debate tumbles along.

Quentin Tarantino was born at Knoxville, Tennessee in 1963. His parents moved to South Los Angeles when he was two years old, and this is where he grew up. In 1985 he was working in Video Archives, a video store at Manhattan Beach, with Roger Avery. Presumably Tarantino was referring to this period in his life when he made the much quoted remark 'I didn't go to film school, I watched movies'. By 1986 he had started to make the film *My Best Friend's Birthday* but it was never finished. In 1987 he wrote the script for *True Romance*, selling it in 1990 for $50,000. A second script, *Natural Born Killers*, was finished by 1988. The money received for *True Romance* was ploughed back into developing his next script *Reservoir Dogs*, a black and white movie shot on 16mm stock. During this project he went to work for an independent Hollywood production company, CineTel, where he met Lawrence Bender. Bender knew a friend of Harvey Keitel's wife and eventually Keitel got to read Tarantino's script for *Reservoir Dogs*. Through Keitel's interest Monte Hellman and Richard Gladstein became involved with the production. In 1991 rushes were shot and important Hollywood names, including Terry Gilliam, started to show interest. The film premiered in 1992 and went on to tour the world festival circuit before Miramax took it up and released it in the US in 1992 and in the UK in 1993.

With the success of *Reservoir Dogs* secured, Tarantino wrote *Pulp Fiction*. The film picked up the Palme d'Or at Cannes and was released in the US on 14 October 1994, the UK 21 October 1994, France 26 October 1994 and Germany on 3 November 1994. It was released in many other countries throughout 1995.

Pulp Fiction grossed $100m worldwide as well as being nominated for Academy Awards for Best Picture, Best Director, Best Actor, Best

Supporting Actor and Best Supporting Actress. *Pulp Fiction* picked up the Oscar for Best Original Screenplay 1994. Had it not been running against *Forrest Gump* for Best Picture it probably could have taken the top prize that year.

Now a prominent figure in Miramax, Tarantino co-wrote and co-directed *Four Rooms* (1995), *From Dusk Till Dawn* (1996), *Jackie Brown* (1998) and *Forty Lashes* (2000).

There are many difficult issues to be addressed in the discussion of the director as auteur, but in the case of *Pulp Fiction* it is not hard to identify some shots and situations that are typical of Quentin Tarantino. Although not previously unseen in the history of Hollywood, the shot that positions the viewer in the boot of a car as it is opened by Vincent and Jules outside Brett's apartment bears the signature of Tarantino. Another example is the triangular (or quadratic) armed stand-off in the final sequence in the diner with Honey Bunny, Pumpkin, Jules and later Vincent. Tarantino was intrigued by this portrayal of apparently unsolvable armed deadlock, and locates the origin of his intrigue in the films of Hong Kong film director Ringo Lam, such as *City on Fire* (1987).

Rather than any particularly discernible essence of originality or authorship it is probably the combination of shots, sets, scenes, soundtracks and situations that come together to give a film the look and feel of a Tarantino movie.

key players' biographies

JOHN TRAVOLTA (VINCENT VEGA)

John Travolta was born in February 1954 at Englewood, New Jersey, USA, first coming to prominence as the arrogant Vinnie Barbarino in the TV series *Welcome Back, Kotter* (1975). In 1977, he launched into a big-screen career with the disco blockbuster *Saturday Night Fever*. Following this box-office and critical success he failed to capitalise on the fame, and did little other than lightweight dramas and minor TV movies throughout the 1980s. He eventually made a comeback in *Look Who's Talking* (1989), then went on to become one of the most bankable male leads in Hollywood after his Oscar nomination for his *Pulp Fiction* role as Vincent Vega.

By October 1997 Travolta was ranked at twenty-one in *Empire* magazine's 'The Top 100 Movie Stars of All Time' list. He was featured on the front cover of *Rolling Stone* magazine on four occasions, the most for any actor during 1994, the year of *Pulp Fiction*'s general release.

It could even be argued that Richard Gere owes his film career to Travolta. Travolta turned down the leads for *Days of Heaven* (1978), *American Gigolo* (1980) and *An Officer and a Gentleman* (1982), and Gere went on to star in each of those films.

Travolta married Kelly Preston twice; the couple met on the set during the filming of *The Experts* (1989). He is a member of the Church of Scientology.

SAMUEL L. JACKSON (JULES WINNFIELD)

Travolta together with Samuel L. Jackson makes an awesome twosome. Jackson, as religious psychopath Jules Winnfield, delivers one of the most powerful soliloquies of menace and madness; a prelude to the violent ironies to come in the film.

Samuel L. Jackson was born in 1948 at Washington DC. During the early stages of his career he was typecast as the bad guy junkie. Nevertheless, his development as an actor later enabled him to transform into an action hero, Mitch Henessey, in *The Long Kiss Goodnight* (1996) and Zeus Carver in *Die Hard: With a Vengeance* (1995). Having recorded these successes he soon graduated from supporting roles to leading man. His performance in *Pulp Fiction* was nominated for an Academy Award.

As a young man Jackson was a leading activist in the black student movement, and in the seventies he joined, together with Morgan Freeman, the Negro Ensemble Company. In the eighties he became well known in a series of three movies made by Spike Lee; *Do the Right Thing* (1989), *Mo' Better Blues* (1990) and *Jungle Fever* (1991). He received a Silver Berlin Bear for his part in Tarantino's movie *Jackie Brown* (1997) playing Ordell Robbi. Jackson was a habitual drug user until he completed a rehabilitation programme just a few weeks before playing a drug addict in *Jungle Fever* (1991).

UMA THURMAN (MRS MIA WALLACE)

As a foil for the gritty pairing of Samuel L. Jackson and John Travolta Tarantino cast Uma Thurman as the enigmatic Mia Wallace. Uma Thurman came to the wider attention of moviegoers in *Dangerous Liaisons* (1988) alongside Michelle Pfeiffer, Glenn Close and Keanu Reeves. The latter years of the nineties saw her career soar after a rather disappointing start in John Boorman's turgid comedy *Where the Heart Is* (1990). Nevertheless, *Pulp Fiction* propelled her on to notable appearances in, for example, *Gattaca* (1997) and the box office smash *Batman & Robin* (1997).

It could be argued that *Pulp Fiction* gave some direction to a career that appeared to be wandering aimlessly in the case of Uma Thurman; with John Travolta the film revived a career that had collapsed into a moribund state.

BRUCE WILLIS (BUTCH COOLIDGE)

Bruce Willis stormed on to the Hollywood scene with *Die Hard* (1988) and instantly became one of the most sought after male leads in the business. His prodigious work rate is clearly demonstrated by his credits in 1994 and 1995: *Die Hard: With a Vengeance* (1995), *Four Rooms* (1995), *Twelve Monkeys* (1995), *Pulp Fiction* (1994), *Colour of Night* (1994), *North* (1994) and *Nobody's Fool* (1994). Clearly 1994 was a busy year for Willis, but more significantly it can be seen as a scoop for Tarantino to have secured such an in-demand star for the role of Butch Coolidge in *Pulp Fiction*.

HARVEY KEITEL (WINSTON WOLF)

Since the success and acclaim of *Reservoir Dogs* (1992) Harvey Keitel seemed to be an automatic selection for anything that Tarantino did next. Keitel, like other members of the cast, has mapped an interesting career through Hollywood. Harvey Keitel was born in 1939 at Brooklyn, New York. He made his initial breaks in the movie industry in the early films of Martin Scorsese: *Mean Streets* (1973) and *Taxi Driver* (1976). However, from the mid-seventies to the mid-eighties he was confined to working mainly in

Tarantino will often appear in his own movies

In the Hitchcockian tradition,
Tarantino (right) will often
appear in his own movies

PULP FICTION

the theatre. His career meandered throughout the eighties, but some commendable performances can be recorded; *Cop Killer* (1983) for example. His most significant role, apart from *The Piano* (1993), was as the menacing Mr White in *Reservoir Dogs* (1992) His most recent appearance has been in the critically acclaimed *Holy Smoke* (2000); a return to the fold of the New Zealand film makers that gave us *The Piano* (1993), Anna and Jane Campion.

narrative & form

narrative summary

Pulp Fiction is divided into five distinct parts:

- Prologue
- Vincent Vega and Marsellus Wallace's Wife
- The Gold Watch
- The Bonnie Situation
- Epilogue

The Prologue includes the discussion between Pumpkin and Honey Bunny about holding up the diner – and their decision to do so. Vincent and Jules go to the flat where their man Marvin is waiting to give them a briefcase for Marsellus.

Vincent Vega and Marsellus Wallace's Wife contains Butch taking the bribe from Marsellus, Vincent buying and sampling the heroin, Vincent's date with Mia, Mia's overdose, and Butch's dream before the fight.

The Gold Watch has Butch cheating Marsellus by winning the fight. He takes flight then returns to his apartment to recover the gold watch that had belonged to his father. Butch kills Vincent who is waiting at the apartment to kill Butch. Butch runs into Marsellus outside the apartment and after a fight they are taken captive by Maynard and Zed. Marsellus is raped before Butch can rescue him. Marsellus repays the rescue by letting Butch go.

The Bonnie Situation returns to the collection of the briefcase and takes up the story from there. Vincent and Jules have a narrow escape from death and Jules is convinced that it was through divine intervention. Vincent and Jules murder the three young men in the apartment. In the car Marvin is accidentally shot in the face and killed by Vincent. Winston Wolf is called in by Marsellus to clear up the 'mess'.

The Epilogue closes the film with Vincent and Jules, having disposed of the cleaned-up car, going for breakfast at the Hawthorne Grill, the diner that Pumpkin and Honey Bunny are planning to hold up. Pumpkin and Honey Bunny hold up the diner, but Vincent and Jules refuse to give up the briefcase. Jules does a deal with Pumpkin and Honey Bunny, and Vincent and Jules leave the diner with the briefcase.

A WORD ABOUT NARRATIVES

Pulp Fiction unfolds three interrelated and interlocking narratives: Honey Bunny & Pumpkin, Vincent & Jules and Butch Coolidge the boxer; but none of the three is told conventionally inside a linear order of events. Tarantino plays with time which leads to the fractured narrative. Because of this unorthodox format *Pulp Fiction* can be found to be difficult to watch. The accepted way of reading a narrative with a beginning, middle and end needs to be relaxed in order to follow *Pulp Fiction*'s internal logic. In conventional film narratives accepting the unreal relationship between film time and real time is one of the concessions that the viewer has to make in order to go along with the telling of the story, and we can all do this without too much difficulty because that is the way we have learned to watch films. However, different concessions need to be made when watching *Pulp Fiction*. For example, the opening scene introducing Honey Bunny & Pumpkin is not resolved until the very end of the film. It can be argued that a film shot with multiple and fractured narratives deliberately renders the film difficult to watch, making it available and interesting to only a minority of film *aficionados*. Furthermore, for a film maker to take great care in ensuring that the initial experience of watching the film is made strange can be interpreted in a political sense by categorising the film as Brechtian. However, *Pulp Fiction* was a popular success both in the USA and the rest of the western world, and box-office receipts demonstrate that the handful of film *aficionados* were joined by millions of others who may have been assumed to be lacking in the cultural capital required to appreciate such a supposedly difficult movie. As for *Pulp Fiction* being Brechtian, it can most certainly be understood from that particular Marxist perspective, but it is doubtful that Tarantino had the slightest intention of grinding any political axes in the making of his picture.

narrative summary narrative & form

monday

Vincent and Jules drive to Brett's apartment

They enter Brett's at about 07.22

Roger and Brett are murdered

At 08.40 Winston Wolf is contracted

Marvin is accidentally shot dead in the car

Vincent and Jules go to Jimmie's

At 08.49 Winston Wolf arrives at Jimmie's

After the clean up Vincent and Jules go to the Hawthorne Grill to eat

At about 9.20 Pumpkin and Honey Bunny pull the hold up

Vincent and Jules leave the diner

At about 10.00 Butch is being bribed by Marsellus at Sally LeRoy's

Vincent and Jules arrive at Sally LeRoy's

Vincent confronts Butch at the bar

tuesday

Evening. Vincent goes to Lance's house to buy heroin

The dance contest at Jack Rabbit Slim's

Vincent picks up Mia for the date

Vincent and Mia go home. Mia overdoses on heroin

Mia is revived at Lance's

16 | PULP FICTION

wednesday

Evening. Butch has a
dream of Captain Koons
before the fight

Butch wins the
fight and escapes
in Esmarelda's cab

Butch has rendezvous
with Fabienne at
River Glen Motel

thursday

Butch and Fabienne
wake up and realise
that Butch's watch
has been left at
his apartment

Butch goes back
to his apartment
to collect his
watch

Butch murders Vincent

Butch heads back to
the motel and meets
Marsellus on the way.
They fight

Butch and Marsellus are
captured by Maynard in
the Mason-Dixon pawn shop

Marsellus is raped by
Maynard's friend Zed

Butch kills Maynard and
rescues Marsellus

Butch returns to Fabienne and they escape

END

confused time lapse

To make a summary of *Pulp Fiction* is a challenging project unless the internal logic of the film is acknowledged, and the authority of that logic is respected. Mapping a movie that does not adhere to the conventions of classic Hollywood narrative requires a slightly different approach which can be graphically explained as shown on pp. 16–17.

Why Tarantino chose to make the film using a fractured narrative technique is a less important consideration than exactly how he broke up the narrative. It is arguable that, as *Pulp Fiction* is a parody of the Hollywood gangster movie, Tarantino decided to make a similar parody of the classic Hollywood narrative form as well, and in doing so he also created a new genre, the postmodern gangster movie. As we shall see later, confused time lapse and setting is a recognisable feature of many films that may be regarded as postmodern.

To explore the final cut in detail it is useful to reconstruct the fractured narrative, reverting *Pulp Fiction* to a classic Hollywood linear narrative. The events in the film take place in a film time continuum starting at about seven in the morning. The key events happen in the following sequence:

linear narrative summary in film time

■ Vincent and Jules travel by car to collect a briefcase from 'our guy'.

■ Vincent tells Jules that Marsellus has told him to take Mia, his new wife, out to dinner that evening.

■ They arrive at the apartment at 7.22 a.m., during further discussion of Mia.

■ They collect the briefcase and its mysterious contents from the apartment, shooting dead three men, one of whom was discovered hiding in the bathroom. A fourth man, Marvin (referred to as 'our man') they take away with them.

■ On the journey back to their boss Vincent accidentally shoots Marvin in the face at point blank range killing him instantly, and making a gruesome mess of himself, Jules and the interior of the car.

dressed comically in tee-shirts and shorts

■ Jules suggests that they divert to the house of a friend to dispose of Marvin's body. Jules's friend, Jimmie, is willing to help them but is alarmed because his wife, Bonnie, is due to return from work in about an hour and a half. It is now 8.17 a.m.

■ Jules calls Marsellus for help. Marsellus calls Winston Wolf (The Wolf) asking him to sort the situation out.

■ Wolf arrives and with method and discipline shows Vincent, Jules and Jimmie how to carry out their task.

■ Now without their bloodied suits, dressed comically in tee-shirts and shorts, Jules and Vincent go to the Hawthorne Grill, a nearby diner, for breakfast.

■ During Jules and Vincent's breakfast Honey Bunny and Pumpkin, who had been planning to rob the diner and its customers, spring the hold-up.

■ While terrorising and robbing customers Pumpkin comes to Jules (Vincent is in the washroom) and demands to see what is in the briefcase. Jules uses the opportunity of showing him to pull a gun and threaten Pumpkin. During a triangular stand-off with pistols poised, Jules convinces Pumpkin and Honey Bunny to make do with the spoils robbed from the other diners and $1500 of his own money. The situation is resolved and Vincent and Jules leave the diner.

■ In a bar where Marsellus is waiting for Jules and Vincent, Butch Coolidge is being bribed by Marsellus to throw a fight. Butch agrees and takes the money.

■ As Butch is leaving, Jules and Vincent arrive to deliver the briefcase to Marsellus. Butch and Vincent have a short and significant menacing exchange.

■ Vincent is becoming apprehensive about his appointment with Mia.

■ Vincent visits Lance, his supplier, to buy heroin. He buys a particularly pure variety that is packaged in the way that cocaine is normally wrapped.

■ Having sampled the 'choco' heroin Vincent goes to collect Mia for their date. Mia and Vincent go to eat at Jack Rabbit Slim's. Mia insists that they enter a twist contest, which they win.

Back at her apartment, while Vincent is in the bathroom, Mia finds Vincent's 'choco' heroin and mistaking it for cocaine, snorts a line. The overdose leaves her unconscious, and on finding her Vincent bundles her into the car to take her to Lance's for an antidote.

At Lance's there is panic that results in the decision to inject adrenaline directly into Mia's heart to revive her. A syringe is plunged through her sternum, she is injected, and she revives.

Back home again, Mia and Vincent agree that the disastrous overdose must not be revealed to Marsellus.

During the same evening as Mia and Vincent's date Butch has a dream while he is relaxing before the fight which he has been bribed to throw in the fifth round. The dream is of the gold watch, a family heirloom that was delivered to him by Captain Koons.

Butch wakes and goes on to win the fight, double-crossing Marsellus. Butch effects his escape in a taxi driven by the strange Esmarelda.

Butch returns to the motel where his girlfriend Fabienne is waiting for him ready to make the escape from the murderous wrath of Marsellus.

The next morning Butch and Fabienne are preparing to bolt when Butch discovers that she has not collected the gold watch from the apartment with the rest of their things. Butch flies into a rage, then decides to take the tremendous risk of returning to collect it.

It is mid-morning when Butch stalks up to his apartment where he can reasonably assume someone will be waiting for him to avenge the double-cross on Marsellus. The apartment is apparently empty, until Butch sees a machine pistol on the kitchen worktop.

Vincent appears from the bathroom expecting the returning visitor to be Marsellus and not Butch. Butch shoots Vincent dead with the machine pistol.

Butch flees from the scene in Fabienne's car, and at a nearby crossroads he confronts Marsellus on a pedestrian crossing. Butch runs Marsellus down then crashes the car. Marsellus and Butch are both injured, but Marsellus chases Butch with a gun.

fractured narrative

■ Butch runs into a pawn shop hoping to trap Marsellus. He succeeds, and they start to fight, only to be stopped at gunpoint by the shopkeeper, Maynard, who takes them captive in the basement. Maynard calls up his friend, Zed.

■ Butch and Marsellus are gagged and bound to chairs by the time Zed arrives. It is decided that Marsellus is the first to be (as we later learn) raped and he is taken away to an adjoining room. Butch manages to remove his bonds and overcomes the bizarre 'Gimp' who is supposed to be watching over him. Choosing a weapon from the store he decides to rescue the unfortunate Marsellus from his attacker. During the rescue Butch kills Maynard. After promising torture for Zed, Marsellus tells Butch that he is free to go, but nobody must hear about the rape.

■ Butch takes Zed's chopper bike and returns to collect Fabienne, then rides off with her on the pillion.

When film is converted back into classic Hollywood narrative it is quite simple and conventionally readable. On closer inspection, some seams and incontinuities are visible, but this is inevitable because the film was not made using the classic Hollywood linear narrative.

fractured narrative summary in film time

PROLOGUE

The action opens after a caption showing the American Heritage Dictionary (New College Edition) definition of the term *Pulp Fiction*.

Honey Bunny and Pumpkin, a couple in their late twenties, are sitting in the Hawthorne Grill having coffee. They are discussing the relative profitability of robbing different sorts of shops and public places. Both are tense and appear to be reassuring each other that the perverse logic of their reckoning is sound. It soon becomes clear that the 'next job' is the diner they are in, the Hawthorne Grill. With chilling and predictable spontaneity they launch into the hold-up. The frame freezes as they leap onto the table pointing their guns at the diners.

There is no establishing shot that leads into this scene, so consequently there is no anchorage for the dialogue. The effect is that the audience is immediately denied their privileged position that the convention of an establishing shot permits; the characters on screen know their location, but the audience does not.

This opening creates curiosity in the audience. They want to know where the diner raid fits in to the overall narrative, and this question remains until the closing scene. They also have the conventional interest in what happens next in the movie.

At this stage it is worth noting that Vincent can be glimpsed walking past Pumpkin and Honey Bunny's table heading for the washroom. An audience making a first viewing of the movie cannot read this glimpse of Vincent significantly in any way. Does this indicate that Tarantino took for granted that the film would be seen by some people again; and indeed, again and again? Through the success of *Reservoir Dogs* (1992), Tarantino had certainly built up a sufficient cult following by 1994 for such an assumption to be made, but that would be rather cynical even by Hollywood standards. Such details, detectable throughout the film, provide both entertainment for the most obsessive and avid cult audience, and they can also be regarded as fine touches on the broader fabric of the whole film. The film can be seen once or even twice as an entertaining piece of gangster action, but further viewing reveals it to be a complex text that can be interrogated academically; indeed, for those so inclined, it can be a personal cultic obsession (see the numerous websites for examples of this mode of consumption). For our purposes here, the details that are useful and relevant to a close analysis in various contexts will be used to build a greater understanding of *Pulp Fiction* in particular and film theory and history in general.

After the credit sequence, the action continues with Vincent and Jules driving to a collection venue to pick something up for their drug dealer boss, Marsellus. Vincent has recently returned from Amsterdam and is discussing some differing aspects of European mass culture with Jules. The dialogue introduces the audience to a range of contradictions and affinities between the two gangsters. Their shared saturation with popular cultural practices, ritual and consumption is at first displayed by a quite detailed discussion of the McDonalds quarter pounder with cheese and how the fast food item is sold and consumed in France. The exchange is resonant of the discussion between Mark Twain's Tom Sawyer and Huckleberry Finn in which they try to fathom how 'foreigners' understand each other taking into consideration the fact that the 'foreigners' speak a foreign language.

```
INT. '74 CHEVY (MOVING) - MORNING
An old gas-guzzling, dirty, white 1974 Chevy Nova
barrels down a homeless-ridden street in Hollywood.
In the front seat are two young fellas - one white,
one black - both wearing cheap black suits with thin
black ties under long green dusters.
Their names are VINCENT VEGA (white) and JULES
WINNFIELD (black). Jules is behind the wheel.
JULES
        Okay, so, tell me again about the hash bars.
VINCENT
        Okay. What you want to know?
JULES
        Hash is legal there, right?
VINCENT
        Yeah, it's legal, but it ain't a hundred
        percent legal. I mean you can't walk into a
        restaurant, roll a joint, and start puffin'
        away. I mean they want you to smoke in your
        home or certain designated places.
JULES
        An' those are hash bars?
VINCENT
        Yeah, it breaks down like this: okay it's legal
        to buy it, it's legal to own it and, if you're
        the Proprietor of a hash bar, it's legal to
```

sell it. It's legal to carry it, but, but, but
that doesn't matter 'cause - get a load of
this, alright - if you get stopped by a cop in
Amsterdam, it's illegal for them to search
you. I mean, that's a right that the cops in
Amsterdam don't have.

JULES

Oh, man, I'm goin', that's all there is to it.
I'm fuckin' goin'.

VINCENT

I know, baby, you'd dig it the most. But you
know what the funniest thing about Europe is?

JULES

What?

VINCENT

It's the little differences. I mean, they got
the same shit over there that they got here,
but it's just, just, there it's a little
different.

JULES

Example?

VINCENT

Well, you can walk into a movie theater in
Amsterdam and buy a beer. And I don't mean
just, like, in no paper cup. I'm talking about
a glass of beer. And in Paris, you can buy a
beer at McDonald's. And you know what they
call a Quarter-Pounder with Cheese in Paris?

JULES

They don't call it a Quarter-Pounder with
Cheese?

VINCENT

No, man, they got the metric system there,

they wouldn't know what the fuck a Quarter
Pounder is.

JULES

What'd they call it?

VINCENT

They call it a Royale with Cheese.

JULES (repeating)

Royale with Cheese.

VINCENT

That's right.

JULES

What'd they call a Big Mac?

VINCENT

Well, Big Mac's a Big Mac, but they call it Le
Big Mac.

JULES

Le Big Mac. What do they call a Whopper?

VINCENT

I dunno, I didn't go into Burger King. You
know what they put on French fries in Holland
instead of ketchup?

JULES

What?

VINCENT

Mayonnaise.

JULES

Goddamn!

VINCENT

I seen 'em do it, man. They fuckin' drown 'em
in that shit.

JULES

Yuck!

mapping her out

This quickfire conversation between Vincent and Jules emphasises their extreme insularity as urban Americans who know or care little about the world outside their own immediate American experience. For Jules and Vincent the concept of non-American, in this case European, can only be considered in the context of an all-American McDonalds quarter pounder with cheese. The discussion of the American quarter pounder and its European counterpart the Royale with Cheese is a demonstration of translating the code of a foreign culture into an American vernacular in order to understand it fully, and only in American terms; an underlying assumption being that before anything makes sense it needs to be Americanised. The burger discussion is a crafted scene that chillingly resonates in the following scene in which Jules verbally humiliates Brett before murdering him.

The conversation between Vincent and Jules serves the purpose of opening the film, introducing two key characters and most importantly creating a mise-en-scène that enables subsequent threads of narrative to unfold. The mundane discussion between the two men lays a thin surface of calm over an underlying tension which is a realistic representation of the mood of two gangsters on their way to a potentially dangerous and violent assignation.

Vincent tells Jules that Marsellus has told him to take Mia, his new wife, out to dinner that evening. They arrive at the apartment at 7.22 a.m., during further discussion of Mia. The theme of American consumer culture continues as Jules explains the character and characteristics of Mia by mapping her out on the terrain of the TV pilot show that she appeared in. Interestingly, Vincent refuses to understand the cipher of popular culture through which he had communicated his European experience to Jules. Perhaps his time in Europe had blunted his skills in translating the unknown into the communicable terms of American popular culture.

As an alternative means of warning Vincent of Mia as potential risk, Jules deploys the code of violence with an anecdote telling how Marsellus punished a man by having him thrown from a fourth storey apartment balcony for giving Mia a foot massage. Vincent immediately understands the message when translated into violent vernacular. The conversation continues with a comic assessment of the erotic status of foot massage compared with other sexual acts. This juxtaposition of violence and comedy sets a pattern of dialogue and situation that persists throughout the film. Mixing violence with humour has the effect of leaving the audience unsure whether they are laughing at the humour of the situation or the violence. It is not normal in mainstream cinematic terms to laugh at violent acts other than those that may be considered 'slapstick' or 'safe violence'. In the earliest traditions of cinema Charles Chaplin insisted that 'kicking asses' was essential to effective comedy, and that tradition persisted until Quentin Tarantino re-wrote the genre of gangster films with *Pulp Fiction*. (See Violence and Humour.)

The foot massage discussion with its juxtaposition of violence and humour is a spoken prelude to the humiliation and murder of the young men in the apartment.

A title card appears to introduce the next episode in the film:

VINCENT VEGA AND MARSELLUS WALLACE'S WIFE

The opening scenes of this episode take place outside and inside Marsellus Wallace's topless bar, Sally LeRoy's. We see Vincent and Jules arrive outside and then enter the bar where they are affectionately welcomed by barman English Dave who, of course, is not English. Butch Coolidge, a boxer, is being told by Marsellus Wallace that he will take a bribe to throw a fight. There is no doubt that Butch has no choice but to take the bribe. The scene is set as an audience with the devil. At times in this scene the camera positions the audience in the seat of the interrogator/inquisitor, Marsellus. An uncomfortable positioning in view of the anecdotal knowledge of Marsellus's propensity towards extreme violence released by Jules in the previous scene. The audience has already been led into conflating the *plaisir* of humour with the *jouissance* of violence, and now it is positioned in the chair of Marsellus/devil. The scene is lit up in a red glare of light in which background objects and scenery bleed into each other; an evocation of the flames of Hell occupied and ruled over by Marsellus. The lighting on

The scene is lit up
in a red glare of light
in which background objects
and scenery bleed into each other

fractured narrative

the face of Butch, in comparison, divides his face precisely down the middle; a dark side and a light side, a visual metaphor for the division of Butch's thoughts. For a professional boxer, being coerced into betraying the values and ambitions he has cherished and trained for throughout his career in the ring by deliberately losing a fight is the ultimate betrayal of prowess and pride. Marsellus explains his demands as a proposition, rationalised by emphasis on the closing stages of Butch's career. Butch is getting too old for the fight game and retirement is imminent, so Marsellus offers a pension scheme he cannot refuse.

The meeting with Marsellus terminated, Butch leaves via the bar of the club. Here there is a strange and chilling exchange with Vincent. It is not at first clear that the two men have met before as they verbally spar in a succinct and threatening way. The most piercing blow, however, is Vincent calling Butch 'Palooka'. The full impact of this insult does not become clear until later on in the film in The Gold Watch, when Butch dreams of receiving an heirloom from Captain Koons, a military colleague of his dead father.

Palooka is another reference to American popular culture; a reference that is almost certainly lost on non-American audiences. Palooka was one of the most famous comic strip characters of the 1940s. Palooka was created by cartoonist Ham Fisher in 1928. As a fifteen-year-old boy he rid his neighbourhood of bullies by beating them up. He matured under the management of his trainer, Knobby Walsh, to become a famous boxing champion. In 1942 Palooka became a celebrated US patriot by stepping down from the ring to enlist as a private in the United States Army. Vincent's comment is the pugilistic equivalent of referring to someone as a Mickey Mouse character. Even in view of the insult Butch's outraged expression appears at first a little excessive. However, the full gravity of the slur is explained later during Butch's dream.

Butch suppresses his anger and the scene fades to another initiating incident in the narrative scheme.

Vincent calls upon Lance to buy some heroin. Jody, Lance's wife, talks avidly to a friend, Trudi, about her passion for body-piercing, as Vincent sits idly but furtively listening to their conversation. As with the Palooka insult the discussion of body piercing initiates an idea that is used later, in the scene where Mia is 'pierced' with the adrenalin injection.

Lance appears and begins to dish out his narcotic goods to Vincent. The sales pitch is woven with constant references to popular cultural artefacts and rituals; The Pepsi Challenge, Baggies and Twistix. The perfect lexicon for selling to Vincent. The deal is done and Vincent buys the purest heroin, choko. As Vincent prepares to sample the choko he and Lance drift into a discussion of the prized possession of the American male, the car. A series of stomach-tightening extreme close-ups of the heroin being prepared and injected cuts to Vincent arriving at Marsellus Wallace's house to take Mia out on the date.

Mia tests, teases and cajoles Vincent throughout the evening that ends with her nearly fatal overdose of choko. (For an in-depth analysis see Contexts: Key Scenes – the date and the overdose.)

THE GOLD WATCH

The following evening sees the boxing match that Butch has been bribed to lose in the fifth round. Fade up to Butch's family living room in 1972. A colleague of Butch's late father, Captain Koons, gives him the watch that has been passed down from his great grandfather. Butch awakes from the dream, distressed and sweating heavily.

He is called to the fight and carries out his deception of Marsellus by winning. He takes flight in a taxi and engages in a strange conversation with the incongruously glamorous driver Esmarelda Villalobos.

Marsellus discovers he has been cheated and vows to wreak revenge on Butch.

Butch arrives at the River Glen Motel where his girlfriend Fabienne is waiting. The following morning as they prepare to complete their escape from the avenging wrath of Marsellus, Butch discovers that Fabienne has forgotten to collect the gold watch that his father passed on to him. Butch becomes hysterical and decides to return to his apartment to recover the watch from the ornamental kangaroo that it had been hung upon for safe-keeping.

Butch approaches the apartment with trepidation because it is likely that Marsellus will have his men waiting for him. On entering the apartment he is perplexed that no one else is there, but nonetheless collects the watch. Oddly, he decides to put two 'toaster pastries' in the toaster. As he does so he notices a gun on the worktop. He realises that there is someone else in the apartment. Vincent emerges from the bathroom thinking that it was Marsellus who had entered the apartment having returned with the ubiquitous fast food snack. Butch kills Vincent with the gun as the toaster pops up.

Making his escape, Butch stops at an interchange, and is startled by Marsellus crossing the road. He attempts to run Marsellus down then drive away, and in doing so crashes the car. They are both injured but Marsellus gives chase. Butch takes refuge in a pawn shop but is cornered and forced to fight Marsellus. Maynard, the shop owner, stops the fight. The two are taken prisoner by Maynard and tied up in the basement of the shop. He calls his friend Zed, who arrives on a chopper. Maynard and Zed intend to use Butch and Marsellus in some kind of sado-masochistic game. Marsellus is chosen as the first 'plaything', and taken bound into 'Russell's old room'. While Marsellus is being raped by Zed, Butch frees himself. He rescues Marsellus, killing 'The Gimp' and Maynard in the process. Marsellus agrees to let Butch go, provided nothing is said of the incident. Butch leaves the pawn shop on Zed's chopper, collects Fabienne and this time makes good his escape.

THE BONNIE SITUATION

At this point the narrative returns to the collection of the briefcase, only this time there is a fourth young man hiding in the apartment nervously listening to the humiliation and murder of Brett. He decides that the only way to escape is to shoot it out with Vincent and Jules, figuring that the element of surprise is in his favour. He jumps out and empties the gun at them. Neither Vincent nor Jules is hit by the point blank salvo, and when the gun is empty they kill the fourth man. Jules sees their survival as an act of God, a Divine intervention.

They take Marvin with them to deliver the briefcase to Marsellus. On the way Vincent accidentally shoots and kills Marvin in the back seat of the car.

72053

There is some panic, and they decide to go to hide the body and clean up the mess at Jules's friend Jimmie's house. At the house, Jules calls Marsellus to ask what should be done, and Marsellus arranges for Winston 'The Wolf' Wolf to sort out the situation before Jimmie's wife Bonnie gets home from work.

The Wolf arrives at the house, as the screen caption says, 'nine minutes thirty seven seconds later'. The Wolf sees that the task of cleaning the car and disposing of the body is done.

EPILOGUE

The job done, Vincent and Jules go for breakfast at the Hawthorne Grill. During their discussion of Jules's decision to quit 'the life' working for Marsellus, Pumpkin and Honey Bunny pull the hold-up.

As they work their way through robbing the diners they get to Jules who reluctantly lets Pumpkin look inside the briefcase (Vincent is in the bathroom). In doing so Jules overpowers Pumpkin and holds a gun to his head. Honey Bunny exchanges the threat with her weapon, and a classic Tarantinian triangular stand-off is formed, just before Vincent returns from the bathroom.

Jules persuades Pumpkin and Honey Bunny to make do with the spoils from the other diners and $1500 dollars of his own, rather than take the briefcase. They agree. Vincent and Jules leave the diner.

narrative as cause and effect

At its simplest narrative is the essential device that articulates incident with incident and conveys something that makes sense. The central enigma of a story may be unravelled by a series of incidental enigmas being solved. The beginning of the film sets the central enigma, the middle solves the interplay between incidental enigmas, and the end resolves the central enigma by answering the questions and tying up all of the loose strands of plot. A basic narrative structure may be as simple as just that, or it may be

refuses to comply with codes and conventions

built upon to take the audience through a highly complex configuration of incidents, blind alleys and red herrings (see *The Usual Suspects* (1995) for example). Within a conventional linear structure one thing happens after the other in a logical pattern of cause and effect. Mystery, suspense, obscurity and puzzlement can all be accommodated but not at the expense of the narrative losing its capacity to make sense.

Some audiences certainly responded to *Pulp Fiction* by saying that it did not 'make sense'. For example, Vincent is shot dead by Butch, then a couple of scenes later he is inexplicably resurrected to apparently re-enact the scene in Brett's apartment that took place near the beginning of the film. Nevertheless, audiences were still able to enthusiastically respond to the episodic events of each fragment of the narrative because they stood up on their own, each containing its own narrative thread. It is something of an achievement to have a film 'make sense' using a narrative pattern that refuses to comply with codes and conventions of traditional linear structure.

Todorov offers a simple framework in which to make an analysis of a film text. It separates the narrative in five separate but related stages: exposition, complication, climax, resolution, and ending. The narrative flow begins with a state of equilibrium, which is then interrupted by events that create conditions of disequilibrium. The action takes place to challenge the disruption and equilibrium is restored, albeit changed by events, but an altered equilibrium nonetheless.

It is difficult to apply Todorovian analysis to Pulp Fiction because of the fractured narrative and disruption in the flow of time. However, taking any one of the three 'stories', for example Honey Bunny and Pumpkin, Todorov's model works as long as we view the 'story' in linear narrative terms. Honey Bunny and Pumpkin in the diner is the first state of equilibrium, disrupted by them pulling the hold-up. The climax is the triangular stand-off before Jules acts to restore order, and a renewed state of equilibrium is achieved as Jules and Vincent leave the diner having thwarted the hold-up.

Propp too looked for a model that could be applied to narrative in order to understand it more fully. Drawing on the tradition of Russian folk tales he

cause and effect   narrative & form

claimed that common structures were shared by filmic texts. Characters would follow a formula according to their function; the hero and the villain, the deceiver or bogus hero, the helpless princess and so on. However a story differed from the next, the underlying structure of character type would be similar. He chose a selection of common situations too; the hero being restricted in some way, the hero reacting to the restriction etc. It is argued that all of Propp's range of situations and characters can be used in the analysis of all texts, but obviously an individual text will not contain all of them. It is more difficult to apply Propp's theories to Pulp Fiction because identifiable character types are in triplicate in the three separate 'spheres of action'.

style

mise-en-scène

Mise-en-scène is a simple concept. It is a French term literally meaning the way the scene is set, from the way a single shot is composed, to the way the whole movie has been put together. However simple the concept may be, making an analysis of mise-en-scène in film studies can become a fascinatingly complex exercise that takes the viewer into a vast constellation of meaning systems. Whatever appears in a scene or a film has been deliberately selected to be there; films are planned, designed and produced with systematic precision. It can be assumed that if something appears in a film it is intended to be there. Of course, there are notable exceptions. For example, one much-celebrated breakdown in continuity, that disrupts the mise-en-scène, happens in *Casablanca* (1942) in the flashback Parisian railway station scene where lovers Rick Blaine (Humphrey Bogart) and Ilse Lund (Ingrid Bergman) part company. There is a torrential rainstorm going on and rain is running heavily off Rick's trenchcoat and trilby hat as he stands on the platform. Cut to Rick having boarded the train; his hat and coat are bone dry.

In *Pulp Fiction* there is a similar inconsistency in continuity. As Vincent drives to the date with Mia a series of ECU shots show the preparation and injection of heroin. The first shots show a metal-tipped syringe sucking up the heroin and then a plastic tipped syringe injecting it. The point to be made here is that those minor inconsistencies, normally only pointed out pedantically, in no way threaten the credibility or readability of the scene or film.

Creating the mise-en-scène is the process of producing the conditions in which the action can be convincingly played out. Mise-en-scène is absolutely essential to mainstream Hollywood cinema because it provides the space in which the realist effect takes place.

To study the way mise-en-scène is created a film can be broken down into its essential parts. For example, the essential elements may be looked at in the following way:

- Setting, set design and location
- Costume and make-up
- Effects (FX) and special effects (SFX)
- Lighting
- Soundtrack & sound
- Screenplay (script)
- Actors' non-verbal communication
- Cinematography
- Temporal flow

Pulp Fiction is an extremely complex film, at times bending the rules of mise-en-scène in order to draw attention to those rules, but it does provide an outstanding opportunity for close textual analysis.

setting, set design and location

The setting of a film is not the same as location. *Casablanca* (1942) was set for the most part in North Africa during the Second World War, but it was a studio-bound production, which means that it was shot entirely in the studio using no outside locations. The dramatic conclusion to *Thelma & Louise* (1991) sees the two women drive their Ford Thunderbird over the edge of the Grand Canyon, but the scene was actually shot in southern Utah.

Pulp Fiction is set in an unremarkable suburban area of an American city. The film does not have any establishing shots that elaborate on this setting, and there is no reference to any particular setting until well into the first thirty minutes when English Dave greets Vincent and Jules at Sally LeRoy's, the topless bar owned by Marsellus. English Dave refers to Jules as 'our man in Inglewood'. Inglewood is a suburb of Hollywood near Los Angeles International Airport. So the precise setting of *Pulp Fiction* is not of crucial importance to what happens in the film. Some films rely heavily on a specific setting to create the essential mise-en-scène. *Manhattan* (1979) for example, was about a TV scriptwriter who had an obsession with New York and New Yorkers, so the setting had to be emphatically identified from the outset of the film. The setting throughout the entire running time of *Pulp Fiction* is left with a non-specific identity.

Set design, however, is considerably more important to creating a mise-en-scène in which to play out the action of *Pulp Fiction*. The film is very 'closed in'; the sets are tightly contained and claustrophobic. This is a device carefully calculated to crank up the intensity required to propagate in the audience the sense of absurdity that is sparked off by the juxtaposition of violence and humour. There is 'nothing' outside the Hawthorne Grill, Sally LeRoy's, Lance's house, Marsellus's apartment, the living room of Butch's childhood home or Esmarelda's cab. The sets are designed to represent heavily stereotyped spaces set in no particular place other than the place in which the action could be credibly expected. This can, of course, work with great effect when unlikely events happen in the most unlikely settings. In Jimmie's suburban backyard amid screen block walls and ornamental shrubs two bloodstained gangsters are washed down with a garden hose by a man in wearing a tuxedo.

The blue sky shots, and there are few, serve only to contrast with a descent into darkness and despair. Butch and Vincent on their way to Brett's apartment cruise through a run-down LA suburb in bright sunlight. They arrive at the apartment block and enter the semi-gloom of the stairwells and landings, before invading Brett's cluttered and curtained room that is to become a death chamber.

Another example of the device of contrasting sunlight with gloom is Butch's flight from his apartment after murdering Vincent. Butch sings along with the car radio; his optimism shines with the sunlit streets leading back to the River Glen Motel where Fabienne is waiting. The plan goes wrong and he finds himself fighting with Marsellus in the cramped interior of Maynard's pawn shop. The next scene in the basement of the store where Marsellus and Butch are bound and gagged is intensified by the confined space and darkness.

Open and closed sets, and light and dark settings are not simply used in contrast but also as sequential devices to help the action develop from the bright open space of day to the intense confinement of horrific darkness.

costume and make-up

Within the sets devised by the designers and location managers the mise-en-scène is developed further by making those appearing in them credible and where necessary incredible.

Costume in *Pulp Fiction* guides the audience towards preferred readings of characters by the use of stereotypes and conventions. It also offers clues to unravelling the fractured narrative. For example Vincent and Jules are wearing shorts and tee-shirts in Sally LeRoy's early in the film. It is only later that we learn the scene takes place in 'real' time after the subsequent events in 'film' time, once we see why Vincent and Jules had to change out of their bloodied suits.

The costumed actors occupy the sets and integrate with the objects placed in the sets and this initial visual statement activates a meaning system in which the narrative can start to unfold. Costume can establish and reinforce details of the set and setting such as period, geographical location, season and climate. Costumes can be abbreviations for class, peer group, nationality and much more besides. In *Pulp Fiction* the costumes of the characters change very little, but the changes of detail are subtle and significant. Pumpkin and Honey Bunny are dressed in the casual summer clothes of young people found in any diner. They are not making threatening non-verbal statements through any particular adornment that may be a label of an aggressive youth cult. This unremarkable image of two youngsters at breakfast makes their conspiracy to rob the diner, that only

No longer dressed to kill,
Vincent and Jules are ironically
wearing clothes similar to
those of their young victims

the audience are privileged to hear, more sinister; more so in the epilogue when they actually launch the robbery.

Vincent and Jules, however, are dressed to kill. Their cheap dark suits and thin black ties generate intertextual meaning with stereotypes of the gangster genre, and particularly with the re-defined gangster stereotypes established in *Reservoir Dogs* (1991). Their change of clothing later on at Sally LeRoy's is not immediately puzzling but more curiously humorous; gangsters look pretty stupid dressed in college kids' clothes. But at the end of the film the grotesque absurdity is compounded by the reason revealed for the change of clothes. Furthermore, the college kids' costume is a thread, or trace, of both what is about to happen and what has already happened in the fractured narrative. With these costumes alone, Tarantino is making a macabre joke by dressing the gangsters in the college kids' uniform of the young men they have just humiliated and murdered.

Other useful examples of how costume can be used to thread together incidents and lay down fine lines of continuity with narrative strands can be identified in the costumes of Jody, Lance's wife, and Mia. When Vincent visits Lance's to buy heroin he eavesdrops on a conversation between Jody and her friend Trudi about body piercing. Jody enthuses over the greater artistic integrity of using a needle to pierce rather than a gun. Jody's enthusiasm for and obsession with body piercing is the backdrop of a subtle but brutal visual joke that is made a few scenes later on. To revive Mia from the heroin overdose she is injected directly into her heart with adrenalin. The sight of this ultimate body pierce appears to be the climax of Jody's entire life as she sees the needle thud through Mia's sternum and into her heart.

As a prelude to this scene, and as a part of the particular narrative strand of the overdose, the twist competition at Jack Rabbit Slim's uses Mia's costume as a way of putting her body directly on to the narrative agenda. Her sexuality and its potentially fatal attraction has already been assessed by Vincent and Jules on their way to Brett's apartment, and her seductive behaviour with Vincent during dinner confirms her dangerous reputation. Up to the scene where she and Vincent toy with their meals, little had been seen of Mia other than a series of extreme close-up shots and head and shoulder medium close-ups. She sat through dinner with her modest white blouse unbuttoned once from the collar. When she appears on the dance floor for the twist competition a second button has been undone, and during the dance she exposes her cleavage focusing attention on the spot that is to become the target of the adrenalin-loaded syringe.

effects (fx) and special effects (sfx)

Pulp Fiction is not a film rich in effects or special effects, but where effects are used they are used with masterful economy. The volume of the gunshots is enhanced and increased just a little more than what would be normal in most action movies to help make the point that the film is a movie about movies and how they are made. The effects are there to draw attention to themselves as effects: the syringe wobbling in Mia's chest and the blood and fluids on her face are realist effects and only ever that. The cut to Butch removing broken windshield glass from his face is made deliberately half a second too late giving away the hand of the effects technician who staged the shot.

Tarantino tends to prefer to keep the effects simple and visible, a device that guarantees impact as well as putting his signature on the movie.

lighting

Lighting is one of the most powerful tools a film maker can use in the process of constructing a mise-en-scène. Paradoxically, natural light such as moonlight or sunlight is rarely of sufficient quality or colour to create a mise-en-scène in which the realist effect can be achieved. Important decisions need to made concerning the type of light used, and there are a mass of choices available ranging from hard light to diffused or soft light. Hard light will produce sharp shadows and vivid images and soft light will mellow the image. This combined with colour and light source provides a huge palette for the lighting cameraman or director of photography. Generally a mainstream film is lit observing the usual film conventions of

lighting

awash in a flood of red

lighting practice; key light, filler and back light with the additional balances achieved by use of kickers. A well-lit set should be naturalistic and able to accommodate the nuances of craftsmanship required to create the illusion of reality: the realist effect. (For further discussion of realism see *Realism*, Linda Nochlin, 1971.) As with all movies the way *Pulp Fiction* is lit is an essential aspect of how the film makes meaning.

For example, the scene in which the audience is introduced to Marsellus Wallace can be described more accurately as the scene in which the audience is introduced to the *idea* of Marsellus Wallace. The generally naturalistic lighting plot of the previous scenes is contrasted with the light set in the bar of Sally LeRoy's. In the genre of gangster movies empty bars and night clubs, the natural lairs of 'main men' and Mr Bigs, are not lit to achieve a natural appearance; the light is normally an exotic cocktail of subterranean colour. And for the first two minutes of Butch's 'audience with the devil' he is awash in a flood of red. The lighting is both realistic in that it is a credible representation of such premises under such circumstances, and it is also an evocative metaphor for the 'heat' being put on Butch. The smouldering cavernous hell from which Marsellus Wallace marshals his troops and manipulates his victims is as inescapable for the audience as it is for Butch. As the scene fades up Butch is already there in front of Marsellus, and at the end of the meeting he does not leave the room. Vincent and Jules are met at the door by English Dave in a daylit shot, but once inside, Marsellus's scarlet control capsule of menace has no easily accessible door or windows. The glow of the red aura of Marsellus's evil spills into every cleft and onto every highlight in the room. Faces, clothes and surfaces bleed into a monochromatic metaphor for malevolence. In this scene Tarantino has taken lighting devices to the extreme, deliberately overcooked a stereotypical lighting plot and turned conventions over by using diffused light to convey menace, evil and absurdity.

sound and soundtrack

It is not always at first apparent whether the soundtrack of *Pulp Fiction* is diegetic or non-diegetic. Diegetic sound is sound that comes from the reality created in the film. For example, as Butch drives away from his apartment for the last time he sings along with music on the car radio; the music on the car radio is diegetic. Non-diegetic sound comes from outside the action, music that helps set an atmosphere. During the murder in the shower scene in *Psycho* (1960), the screaming violins are non-diegetic.

At the beginning of the scene in Sally LeRoy's for nearly two minutes the camera is on Butch in a medium close-up shot of his head and shoulders. A voice (the audience does not yet know that it is the voice of Marsellus) is telling Butch with brutal frankness and authority that his career as a professional boxer is nearing its end. It is not clear throughout the monologue if the voice is diegetic or non-diegetic. It could be Butch's own inner thoughts being spoken as a voice-over but the camera is just a couple of degrees off being a point of view shot and positions the audience at the shoulder of whoever Butch is being addressed by. The camera and the mysterious voice pin Butch down. The non-diegetic soundtrack, Al Green's *Let's Stay Together*, is cued in with the title card 'Vincent Vega and Marsellus Wallace's Wife' providing a placid underlay to an intimidating speech. The encounter is taking place in a 'non-space' until a bag of cash comes into shot, offered teasingly by the 'voice'. The scene is still timeless and in a 'non-space' until the audience is repositioned by cutting to reverse field shot over the shoulder of Marsellus. It is the soundtrack that anchors the scene back into a comfortable and familiar viewing position for the audience. Butch agrees that in the fifth round of the fight his 'ass goes down'; cut to English Dave opening the door to welcome Vincent and Jules. The Al Green soundtrack becomes diegetic because it can be heard coming from inside the bar with realistically diminished volume as English Dave opens the door, and then with increased volume as ambient sound on the cut to Vincent and Jules entering Sally LeRoy's. The thread that linked the unreal, non-space scene of the bribe to the central narrative was the soundtrack shifting from non-diegetic to diegetic. The audience is comfortably re-positioned to see the narrative unfold further.

Soundtrack and sound are probably the least 'visible' aspect of any film; the fine touches of continuity and referencing that they add are barely noticeable but the text in its entirety would suffer without them. Take, for example, the short clip of Butch circumnavigating the neighbourhood on his way back to his apartment to collect his watch. Moving down a path by the side of a house a radio can be heard through an open window advertising 'Jack Rabbit Slim's'. Butch glances cursorily and continues on his way.

screenplay (script)

The screenplay is the embryo from which the film develops. It is rare for the final release cut look like the first-draft screenplay. Several drafts or re-writes will evolve from the first before a final screenplay, or shooting script, is arrived at. And even then a shooting script is open to interpretation.

Pulp Fiction won a US Academy Award for Best Screenplay in 1994. Adulation and awards are not given after close examination of the original script, because screenplays are not works of literature and were never meant to be; they are much more than that. Screenplays are blueprints used in a vast process of production that results in a film.

The script is the backbone of the screenplay. The language of *Pulp Fiction* is of the LA streets; it conveys threat and menace with humour, and humour with threat and menace. At times, however, the language becomes poetic. For example, in the scene where Vincent calls at Marsellus's house to pick up Mia for their date at Jack Rabbit Slim's they share an exchange over the intercom. The speech pattern of their brief conversation has an underlying structure of words ending with the 'o' sound: fellow, disco, hello, hello, let's go. This one of the most obvious patterns to identify, and there are many others coming in a multitude of formations. They are best analysed by listening first and if necessary by reference to the script, but it is important to remember that meaning systems that are set up in films are to be studied only in a filmic context; screenplays and scripts are never meant to stand alone as literary texts.

The tone of the script will vary too, and just as in the real world of everyday linguistic encounters resonance, congruence and dissonance occur. Some critics have pointed out that the amount of 'foul' language used in *Pulp Fiction* is excessive. In doing so they have made the indication that they have been listening selectively, only hearing the profanities. The richness of the urban argot provides a versatile vocabulary appropriate to those who need to communicate successfully and survive in the sub-cultures that exist in the diverse and complex configurations of the modern world. *Pulp Fiction* is about criminal sub-cultures and any attempt to bowdlerise the language would destroy its brutal lyricism.

To examine the language of the film in sufficient depth attention needs to be paid at least to content, structure, pace and rhythm. Speeches made by Marsellus to Butch in Sally LeRoy's, and to Zed in the basement of Maynard's pawn shop have the powerful warped logic resonant of King Lear. Jules's ranting recitations are in a way more biblical than actual quotations from the Bible, and the lovers' plans and aspirations shared between Pumpkin and Honey Bunny and Butch and Fabienne are ageless, timeless and as hopelessly touching as those uttered by Trevor Howard and Celia Johnson in *Brief Encounter* (1945) over half a century ago. For further discussion of language and popular culture see Narrative & Form.

actors' non-verbal communication

Although non-verbal communication includes such detail as costume, hair, make-up and jewellery a great deal of information is passed specifically through body language. Facial expression, gesture, posture, gait and so forth enable the actor to convey a range of meanings as an abbreviation of dialogue, or as an enhancement to spoken lines. An example of intense expression is the short encounter between Vincent and Butch in Sally LeRoy's. A minimal amount of dialogue is exchanged between the two but the intensity of the meeting is cranked up from simmer to just short of boiling by Butch's facial response to being called 'Palooka' and 'punchy'. The overall 'enclosed' quality of *Pulp Fiction* is contributed to by the proxemics of the actors; they are generally very close to each other. At times Vincent and Jules are so close they border on the comic by collapsing their individual personal space bubbles into one. This is put to good effect in the scene featuring their literally and metaphorically close discussion of Mia outside Brett's apartment.

framing of the action

the shot and edit

The shots and editing used in *Pulp Fiction* are complex. The clever cuts used to such great effect in films such as *The Matrix* (1999) are not seen in *Pulp Fiction*. Tarantino has a style that creates its effect with the audience hardly noticing what has been done; like lighting, shot selection can be 'invisible'. Tarantino's use of the extreme close-up (ECU) is probably the most powerful shot in his director's armoury. The ECUs used to explore Mia before we have seen her full-face (as she conducts her secret surveillance of Vincent), give the audience the opportunity to become intimately involved with the (so far) unfamiliar.

In one of the most bizarre sequences, the murder of Vincent, Butch re-enters his apartment to recover the watch. An ECU shot of his key entering the lock deploys the standard device designed to build tension. Butch then puzzlingly decides to prepare himself a 'toaster pastry', a very odd thing to do in view of the strong possibility of an ambush. The scene briefly becomes a parody of TV advertising as there is a fast cut to an ECU of the 'toaster pastry' packaging imitating the standard product image shot which is the cornerstone of any good advertisement. Also this fast cut to ECU is a typically Tarantinian reference to the growth in product placement in mainstream Hollywood movies. *Pulp Fiction* is a film made almost entirely from medium shots, medium close-up and close-up woven together with fast cuts to extreme close-up. It is difficult to find even a handful of medium long shots.

The framing of the action in *Pulp Fiction* is remarkable. While it is best appreciated watching under normal circumstances, it is best observed for its technical excellence with the sound off. In the scene at the River Glen Motel where Butch and Fabienne wait to make their escape, Butch becomes transfixed by a violent scene from the film *The Losers* (1970) showing on the TV. The TV is seen full frame, and to the left Fabienne's reflection can be seen hovering spectrally on the TV screen.

director's cuts

There are two main scenes that were lifted and do not appear in their original form in the general release: Vincent arriving at the Wallaces' apartment to take Mia out on the date, and Butch escaping in the taxi with Esmarelda.

The scene with Vincent arriving to take Mia out was a very different sequence from the final cut. It opened with Vincent arriving at the apartment. He is seen through a hand-held Hi-8 video camera. The shots have the camera-shake and haphazard framing that is typical of the impromptu home-shoot, and are eerily voyeuristic. It becomes clear that Mia is videoing an interview with Vincent aiming to find out what sort of person is taking her out to dinner; and indeed, to determine if he is a an acceptable escort. From Mia's point of view, through the Hi-8, Vincent is trapped; cut to Mia in medium close-up from Vincent's point of view shooting him through the Hi-8. The audience has not seen Mia's face; we can only hear her interrogation of Vincent as she shoots. The point of view shifts from video to film; from the faceless Mia to Vincent pacing like a trapped beast pinned down by the lens; Mia is in control and Vincent is squirming. She conducts the interrogation after reassuring Vincent not to worry, and to 'pretend I'm Barbara Walters' (Barbara Walters being an anchor-person on the TV news and features programme 'The View' produced by ABC Daytime and Barbara Walters' Barwall Productions). Vincent is cornered. Unable to solve this situation by threat or violence, he is being playfully grilled by Marsellus Wallace's wife, and he responds uncomfortably and monosyllabically. Nobody else would be allowed to get away with subjecting Vincent to such a humiliation. However, Mia is in control, playing and happy. The questions she confronts Vincent with are strange:

MIA

      ... Are you any relation to Susanne Vega?

VINCENT

      Yeah, she's my cousin.

MIA

      Susanne Vega the folk singer is your cousin?

Using the technique of a trained interrogator, Mia composes the next question from the last answer, the tactic being to cast doubt about the answers by raising further questions from them; all aimed at eroding the confidence of the interviewee. Mia has a plaything, a dangerous toy with whom she can do whatever she wants without risk.

Vincent, still in Mia's gaze through the Hi-8 lens, is told by Mia, and we still haven't seen her face, that she divides the world into two groups, Elvis people and Beatles people. This explains her puzzling comment outside Jack Rabbit Slim's that 'an Elvis man will love it'. She qualifies her taxonomy by musing that 'Beatles people can like Elvis, and Elvis people can like The Beatles, but nobody likes them both equally'. Vincent becomes more at ease with this question because the universality of popular music culture and its greatest icons are the lingua franca in a world populated by Beatles people and Elvis people; so Vincent scents safer, more familiar territory. The following questions all draw on an assumed knowledge and appreciation of American media culture. Vincent is asked which he prefers, 'Brady Bunch' or 'The Partridge Family'; he answers 'Partridge Family', adding sagely 'There's no comparison' as if he had spent some time on a previous occasion comparing and contrasting the relative merits of the two. Now confidently on the familiar territory he had scented, he responds with greater ease to the 'Rich Man, Poor Man or Archie' question. The 'safe' questions are a deceptive medium for the more barbed questions: 'Your favourite way to say thank you in a foreign language?' forces Vincent to say thank you in a foreign language to a dominant female stranger in gratitude for nothing at all. The other question outside the 'safe' sphere of popular culture, 'Are you a listener or a talker?', is parried by Vincent with the neutral reply that he 'waits to talk'. Vincent eventually passes the test by answering the last glibly offered question, 'If you were Archie, who would you fuck first Betty or Veronica?'. Mia is satisfied with her date and ends the interrogation in the language of film making, 'Cut, print. Let's go eat'. For the first time we see Mia, an erotic siren who looks as tantalisingly dangerous as her reputation.

In an interview about this scene Tarantino said that it was lifted because the use of Hi-8 transferred to film, and Mia as film maker voicing over as she shoots, was what a lot of new directors were doing in the early 90s. Because he did not want it to look that way it was completely re-shot.

director's cuts

The second major lift from the general release cut was Butch's flight from the fatal fight in a taxi with the mysteriously exotic cab driver Esmarelda Villalobos. The release cut with the shorter taxi scene can be seen as an intertextual reference to Scorsese's *Taxi Driver* (1976), as well as a narrative device. The scene as it appears in the release cut serves the purpose of the narrative sufficiently. The extended scene that was cut down contains, perhaps most significantly, a discussion between Esmarelda and Butch about the meaning of her name. 'Esmarelda Villalobos', we are told, means 'Esmarelda of the wolves': her name is Spanish yet she is Colombian. When she asks Butch what his name means (and this part of the dialogue is left in the final release cut), he responds 'I'm an American honey, our names don't mean shit'. The cultural contrast between names and meaning is lost in the final release cut, yet we are still left with the assertion that American names have lost touch with their roots: they too have become 'pulp fiction'.

contexts

key scenes

In such complex texts as feature films it is tempting to separate ideological representations under neat headings; race, class, nationality, gender and so forth. This type of taxonomy can be of use, but it can also underemphasise or fail to acknowledge the complex process of how each representation interacts with the others. For example, the connotations of the term 'nigger' have evolved a long way since its use in the stories by Mark Twain set in the American Deep South at the end of the nineteenth century. Yet Jules, a black man, uses it several times, each time with a differing nuance barely discernible to the ears of non-black non-American audiences. The contemporary use of the term 'nigger' by a black man or a white man, referring to a black man or one of mixed race (Jules refers to Antwan Rockamora or Tony Rocky Horror as a 'nigger' and he was half Samoan, half black) is a socio-anthropological minefield and only safely located when it is set into the context of a film like *Pulp Fiction* in which black men appear to hold the key to the narrative. In *Pulp Fiction* black men do appear to hold the key to the various episodes of the fractured narrative, but closer analysis suggests that the character Butch, the 26-year-old white fighter, is the most significant determinant, either directly or indirectly, in most events.

The themes and contexts, social, cultural and political, can best be explored by a concentrated study of some key scenes.

COLLECTING THE BRIEFCASE

Although this scene is divided in film time it is worth looking at rejoined. The journey to Brett's apartment is our initial introduction to the two central characters Vincent and Jules. As with the previous scene at the

key scenes

Hawthorne Grill there is no establishing shot, but the audience is 'going' somewhere with the two in the car, so the scene is less enigmatic. The dialogue gives little away about the destination, but does release information about Vincent and Jules. Their bizarre yet mundanely conducted discussion of European eating habits heightens the tension because it is in contrast to their appearance as gangsters on a job, and this is just the first notch in the narrative machinery that cranks the tension up. At the end of the discussion the scene fades then comes up again in a typical Tarantino cut; the audience has point of view from the boot of the car as the lid is lifted to reveal Vincent and Jules unloading their weapons. The idea of a body or prisoner being in the trunk and the audience being positioned thus cannot be discounted as just a technique; the shot and cut is a macabre joke.

Their journey to the job and the discussion that they have on the way could have taken place anywhere between two men on their way to the workplace, but their clothing and the audience's intertextual reading of this as a Tarantino gangster movie is a source of audience expectation. The tools of the trade, the weapons, as they are removed from the boot, transform the apparently mundane to the extraordinary.

The conversational exchange between Vincent and Jules as they approach the day's work serves three important purposes. Firstly, it reveals the nature of the relationship between them. Vincent has just returned from an extended period in Amsterdam, yet the two of them are able to converse at ease and in the relaxed manner of those who are in close day to day contact. A measure of the depth and integrity of a friendship is how easily things fall back to the level of affability and familiarity that existed before a prolonged separation. The sexual intimacy of the discussion between them suggests a 'male' closeness that is profound. For example, Vincent can comfortably, but safely, torment Jules by asking, 'would you give me a foot massage?'. A dangerous jibe unless he is sufficiently confident in Jules's tolerance afforded through friendship and affection.

Secondly, the dialogue introduces to the narrative the *idea* of Marsellus Wallace and his wife Mia. Marsellus, their boss, is portrayed as a mythological figure in the Los Angeles underworld, notorious and feared for his capacity for violence; or less directly his ability to command his men to carry out extreme retribution. The punishment suffered by Tony Rocky Horror for allegedly massaging Mia's feet is extreme. The chilling anecdotal mythology of the cruelty and ruthlessness of Marsellus also introduces the *idea* of Mia, his new wife. Furthermore, it also initiates the tension of the potential danger in which Vincent is soon to be put during his date with Mia. This aspect of the exchange is part of the slow exposure of Mia and Marsellus who are only known to the audience by their reputed exploits and attributes.

Thirdly, the mise-en-scène is created to enable the subsequent strands of narrative to unfold. As Jules and Vincent continue the rapid-fire chit-chat it is arguable that the two are biding their time, like soldiers waiting to go 'over the top'. Oddly, Vincent checks his watch with the precise report that it is 'seven-twenty two in the a.m'. This is another notch on the scale of tension, and also a source of humour. There is no apparent reason why they should delay entry to the apartment. If it were apprehension then the continuation of the foot massage discussion would be absurd; and indeed that is exactly the effect aimed at. These postmodern gangsters are neither real nor realistic; they are cinematic signs triggering off irony on top of irony. The characters are from the outset metaphors for realistic representations of hit-men from the entire history of gangsters in the movies; from the swarthy villains of the silent era through James Cagney, George Raft, Edward G. Robinson et al, to the modernist film noir creations of the 1940s and 1950s. *The Godfather* (1972) punctuated the end of the gangster genre.

Having had enough of their speculations on the delights and dangers of Mia Wallace, Jules and Vincent decide to get on with the job, plundering the clichés ('lets get into character', 'let's go to work') as they go.

The comic dialogue that has been spun by the opening scenes is now juxtaposed with an entirely different atmosphere.

INSIDE BRETT'S APARTMENT

Having snapped into character Vincent and Jules amble into the apartment, Jules the interrogator, Vincent the silent, menacing presence.

key scenes

The interrogation has three major phases through which Jules builds himself up into a lethal frenzy. As ever, the leitmotif of consumption and brand labels peppers the monosyllabic patter of intimidation. Phase one: the Kahuna Burger. The minor irritation inflicted by taking Brett's burger is the first step of Jules's onslaught. Spoken in the style of a TV advertisement voice-over Jules announces the slogan 'Hamburgers: the cornerstone of any nutritious breakfast!'. He bites into Brett's burger with the enthusiasm of Homer Simpson, declaring 'Ummmm, that's a tasty burger'. Furthermore, he draws on his newly acquired knowledge and questions Brett on the Royale with Cheese. Brett unwittingly falls into a trap by answering with misjudged alacrity a question Jules himself was unable to fathom earlier, in the car. It is unclear whether Vincent and Jules intended to just recover the briefcase and frighten the young men, or intended to kill them from the outset. Having made the recovery, Jules gets right back into the spiral of humiliation that he had started by commandeering Brett's Kahuna Burger.

It is important to note at this stage the significance of the briefcase. The contents of the briefcase are the subject of great mystery, speculation and debate among the cult followers of *Pulp Fiction*, but there are just two points to be made in this analysis. The briefcase and its contents are a part of the mise-en-scène that enables the fractured narrative to develop. If it is viewed as part of a classic realist narrative it would function to bring characters into contact with each other, and resolve incidental enigmas that run along with the central enigma of the narrative discourse. In the case of *Pulp Fiction*, there is no coherent central narrative, so the puzzle of the narrative itself is part of the central enigma. Also, the content of the briefcase is the object of desire and the 'mysterious' golden light that radiates from it when the briefcase is opened is a reference to an advertising technique. The ubiquitous device in TV advertising determines the product to be an object of desire and floods it in glaring light; the refrigerator door opens and the light is magnified as it bathes the mayonnaise jar in glorious golden light; the couple sitting in a darkened room in front of TV open the box of chocolates to reveal shafts of light, even outshining the glare of the TV screen. Vincent opening the briefcase at the boys' apartment is Tarantino's first deliberately overstated reference to the fantasy world of TV advertising and visual media culture.

The second phase of the terrorisation is the shooting of Roger. This casual action (Jules does not even look at Roger as he shoots him) rapidly escalates the situation from mockery to murder in just a few words and a gesture. Jules verbally pounds Brett with dares to repeat the word 'what' again. The cloying, persuasive language of ad-speak juxtaposed with the violence of LA street talk jolts the audience into that tight corner of discomfort as violence and humour are conflated.

Amazingly Jules turns to the Bible for third phase of humiliation. Having shot Brett in the shoulder Jules continues the interrogation, which has elevated to a higher level of menace and foreboding. Again the Tarantinian juxtaposition discomforts the audience by combining the profane and sacred in one terse line: 'Yes ya did Brett, ya tried to fuck 'im. You ever read the Bible, Brett?' The prolonged ranting speech that is delivered more like a soliloquy than a monologue is recalled by Jules as Ezekiel 25:17. It is not an accurate quotation, but in true postmodern style, it has the appearance of a biblical passage, and the content is an eclectic selection of ideas taken from that Bible and wrought into a terrifying speech. It is worth quoting in full:

JULES

> The path of the righteous man is beset on all
> sides by inequities of the selfish and the
> tyranny of evil men. Blessed is he who, in the
> name of charity and good will, shepherds the
> weak through the valley of darkness, for he is
> truly his brother's keeper and the finder of
> lost children. And I will strike down on thee
> with great vengeance and furious anger those
> who attempt to poison and destroy my brothers.
> And you will know my name is the Lord when I
> lay my vengeance upon you.

key scenes

'Die you motherfuckers ... Die!'

'What just happened here was a fuckin' miracle'

chilling and surreal extreme close-up

Brett is murdered as the scene fades out. There is an overlap when the action is taken up later in the film. Jules is reciting his biblical passage. Another man, a fourth man, is hiding in the bathroom. His only escape is to shoot his way out. The scene is the moment of Jules's transformation; he is convinced that he and Vincent survived the hail of bullets through divine intervention. While Jules is recovering from the holy experience, Vincent uses his knowledge of coincidences and extreme phenomena drawn from the docusoap 'Cops', saying 'This shit happens'.

The accidental killing of Marvin is paradigmatic of the use of irony in the film. Extreme violence in the apartment, the perpetrators redeemed by divine intervention, the revelation to Jules; blasphemy and piety converge as Marvin is accidentally shot in the face.

The key themes of loyalty, retribution and redemption have been set up and the device conflating humour with violence has been introduced and demonstrated with some force. The next section, 'Vincent Vega and Marsellus Wallace's Wife', opens up the new opportunities in the narrative.

THE DATE AND THE OVERDOSE

The scene cuts from a chilling and surreal extreme close-up of Vincent's blood shooting back into the syringe mixing with the choko, to the extreme close-up Vincent's face driving to the date.

Vincent then walks to the door of Mia's house, and the audience view the scene from Vincent's point of view. He picks the note from the door. It reads, 'Hi Vincent, I'm getting dressed. The door is open. Come inside and make yourself a drink. Mia'.

As he/we read the note Mia provides a voice-over. From this point Vincent is under surveillance. The convention of women in movies being generally pinned by the gaze of men is reversed. Dusty Springfield fades up on the soundtrack. The movie camera and security video technology combine to scrutinise Vincent. Women being the subject of close scrutiny by the male voyeur have been the norm since movie reels first rolled. As Laura Mulvey's landmark article, 'Visual Pleasure and Narrative Cinema' argues, 'In a world ordered by sexual imbalance, pleasure in looking has been split

key scenes

between active/male and passive/female' (Mulvey, 1989). Since the early 1970s avant-garde feminist film makers (Laura Mulvey, Sally Potter) have examined the possibilities of shifting the male codes of camera conversations and the grammar of edit.

Mainstream Hollywood has engaged to some extent with the issues of gender and film, but little has changed. Even in apparently campaigning feminist narratives like *Thelma and Louise* (1992) the subject is to do with male power, and men hold the key to the narrative. Also in *Thelma and Louise* a security video is used as a device to create the realist effect and also to further pin down the female fugitives when they taint the male code of violence in holding up a convenience store (see Donald & Scanlan, 'Hollywood Feminism? Get Real', 1992).

We don't see Mia's face as she sits at the control panel of the Wallace house security system. The shots of a man under female surveillance, an apparent reversal of classic realist narrative are confused by the cuts to extreme close-ups of erotic, phallic symbolism: Mia's red lips and the mike, Mia's manicured hands on the joystick. As Mia tracks Vincent the audience, through the 'male' lens, gazes at Mia with her lips in tighter focus than even the human eye could achieve; an invasive shot perfected by (and essential to) that other side of Hollywood, the multi-million dollar porn film industry.

Tarantino plays with conventions and the expectations of the prying audience; Mia's full face has not yet been seen. Her presence excites Vincent; an interesting shot of Vincent standing facing away from a portrait of Mia gives her incidental presence unknown to him. The portrait is a kitsch representation, yet her reclined pose recalls the classical tradition of female figure painting, as does the modest gesture with her right hand. She gazes at the cigarette. The colour is garish and the technique is appropriately clumsy. Kitsch and classical are mockingly juxtaposed to evoke the most tantalisingly grotesque image.

From the control panel Mia cuts a huge line of cocaine and stoops to block the screen, concealing the snort. The music builds as another extreme close-up follows the bare footfall of Mia walking to introduce herself to Vincent. An extreme close-up as the stylus lifts from the vinyl cutting the music off. 'Let's go,' says Mia in the final rhyme of the dialogue that they have exchanged throughout the scene. Mia's feet are simultaneously menacing – remember the cost of the foot massage – and erotic; another destabilising juxtaposition.

JACK RABBIT SLIM'S

Mia and Vincent's opening dialogue introduced a forced intimacy and continues in the Jack Rabbit Slim's scene where, at times, it achieves the 'Hi honey, I'm home' resonance of a domestic low-budget sit-com. The arrival at Jack Rabbit Slim's is the beginning of a scene that should be remembered as a paradigm of postmodern cinema. In the teasing accusation of Vincent being a square, Mia is seen drawing a dotted line between herself and the audience. An emphatic technique used by TV advertising from the 1950s onwards, the device is simple and in the visual vernacular of its own genre can be passed without much impact. But used in a film that has so far parodied numerous techniques of classic realist cinema it is sufficiently destabilising to prepare the audience for Jack Rabbit Slim's.

Jack Rabbit Slim's is the kind of diner that had sprung up all over the USA by the early 1990s. A temple of homage to consumerism and American popular culture: the whole movie is epitomised by the experience and action in Jack Rabbit Slim's. Outside its neon sign has a strap line proclaiming the diner as 'The next best thing to a time machine.' Vincent leads the audience into the diner. He is perhaps a little confused by the neon, plastic, glass, and mirrors that bleed into one another. The walls are covered by 1950s movie posters; *Rock All Night*, *Motorcycle Gang* and *Attack of the Fifty Foot Woman*. TV and movie characters abound, floating holographically and waiting at tables. Zorro, James Dean, Dean Martin, Jerry Lewis and Marilyn Monroe have been plundered from the Pandora's box of American media culture and recreated to the strains of Ricky Nelson. Even the freeway, that most functional sculpture defining the freedom of America, is miniaturised and brought inside to pass through and fly over the diners as they sit at the customised-car tables. The American social and cultural ritual of visiting the diner positions the audience in

key scenes

what Vincent describes as a 'wax museum with a pulse'. The waiting staff play their parts; Marilyn finds an up-draft for her skirt and the Philip Morris Midget scuffles into the neon flood paging 'Mr Philip Morris' like a demented R2D2. The diners fall into their role in the spectacle with hideous ecstasy: this is precisely the case as Mia and Vincent take to the floor in the twist contest. The cynical wisdom and sit-com banality of their conversation over dinner is suspended as they melt effortlessly into the game. They address each other as appropriate before a dance, then as if a switch has been thrown, embark upon a bizarre display of sleaze and sexiness, which combine to create a dance of grotesque elegance.

Postmodern eclecticism is most visible at this point as the overweight psychopath Vincent arrives as John Travolta. Not John Travolta the resurrected and recreated star of *Pulp Fiction*, but John Travolta as Tony Manero from *Saturday Night Fever* (1977). The effect is hyperreal; a movie from the actor's past re-appears intertextually to feed significantly into a movie made almost twenty years on.

BUTCH'S DREAM

Butch's dream before the fight contains a vivid panorama of nostalgia, nationalism, racism and politico-militarism.

The action fades up to a garish extreme close-up of the 1960's children's TV cartoon *Clutch Cargo,* then cuts to Butch as a five year old in the living room of his family home in Alhambra, California. A child feeding on pulp cartoon culture. The cartoon clip continues to play as Mrs Coolidge leads Captain Koons in. The cartoon depicts a mocking stereotypical image of a Native American or Innuit person using stumbling, heavily accented English to humiliate a dog that thinks a totem pole is alive. As Butch switches off the TV a square-jawed, white American male comes into shot. (Many audiences will react with recollection of the actor Christopher Walken as the Mafioso interrogator in Tarantino's *True Romance* (1993), another example of the deliberate manipulation of intertextuality.) The racist connotations of the short cartoon clip brings together four levels of intellect: the inanimate object mistaken as being alive by the incogitant animal, in turn being betrayed by the ethnic animation (the innuit) as a 'funny city dog' to the white American boy who is at the top of the register. This clip, visually grotesque as it combines a filmic/human mouth with an animated face, sets the scene for Captain Koons's monologue on white American family heritage. As with other lengthy monologues the audience is positioned at young Butch's point of view later intercut with extreme close-ups of Captain Koons, Butch and the gold watch.

Captain Koons's avuncular manner softens the authority of his Air Force uniform. He immediately casts himself as surrogate father by telling Butch that he and his father 'were in that Hanoi pit of hell over five years together'. The audience, positioned as they are, cannot fail to trust and admire Captain Koons; his credentials are Vietnam Veteran, comrade in arms of Butch's father, and Officer of the United States Air Force. White, military male, middle-class America addressing the future of the union – young Butch, a child about to be given the token of his responsibility to the future pursuit of the American Dream. Butch has been assured that he will never have to suffer as his father and Captain Koons did at the evil hands of Communism in a Hanoi Prisoner of War camp. But the deal has to be struck that Butch in return must continue the fight to uphold the values and tradition that Koons is about to explain. The watch is shown briefly, then Captain Koons embarks on an emotional account of its pedigree. It is a lesson of American history. Butch's great-granddaddy Private Doughboy (American Infantryman) Ernie Coolidge is the first marker in the line. The watch left the USA with him as he went to fight in Europe in the First World War. The watch is a relic of the Industrial Pioneers of America – it was among the first wristwatches manufactured in the USA.

It is a telling detail in the script that Captain Koons recalls that Doughboy Ernie Coolidge 'sets sail for Paris'. This is an indication of American parochialism. Paris, France is probably as geographically familiar as it could afford to be to the average American in reference to a location outside the USA. Normally a person with any vague knowledge of a foreign country would refer to the port destination in that country, Le Havre, Calais, Cherbourg, etc., but in this case Paris, France is as accurate as can be or

key scenes

needs to be. Jules's fascination with the European experience recounted by Vincent is echoed in this line. It could be an intentional representation of American parochialism, or simply Tarantino writing as a parochial American himself.

The watch as an icon of family comradeship, obligation and responsibility is next deployed when again Americans are called beyond their shores to fight in foreign lands: the Second World War. Butch's grandfather, Dave Coolidge, was the next generation bearer of the token timepiece that gathers another layer of mythological significance. Dave Coolidge died at Wake Island. The full impact of the massacre at Wake Island is probably lost on non-American audiences. In December 1941, shortly after the Japanese air attack on Pearl Harbour, 500 US Marines died in a repulse led by US Marine Commander James Devereux. It is remembered as one of the most heroic stands in US Military history. This reference fixes Dave Coolidge indubitably as an American war hero. So the watch was passed on to Butch's father who was subsequently shot down over Hanoi and died as a Prisoner of War.

The history of the watch is a relic of US military stoicism, comradeship and courage in the face of both victory and tragic loss. Just as Tarantino leads us from humour into violence and in doing so conflates and confuses the boundaries, here too he positions the audience in awe of the American dream then plunges the illusion into absurdity. Butch's birthright, an icon of the American Dream, the gold watch; was stored 'in the one place he knew he could hide something – his ass'.

This killing punchline displaces the dignity and gravity of the monologue that has been built up by conventional realist techniques such as the gradual increase in the extremity of close-up, and the expectation of the audience is not paid off as it would be normally in classic realist texts. The audience is confused and resorts to laughter, at first not being sure what they are laughing at. As with the shooting of Marvin later in the film, the realisation of the source of their amusement causes an uncomfortable thrill, or *jouissance*. Tarantino is not content with that easy success in causing confusion, he applies further outrage by recalling that Dave Coolidge died of dysentery, implying that frequent repeated insertion of the gold watch would be necessitated by such a condition. Dangerously courting overkill, Captain Koons admits to 'my ass' being the final repository of the gold watch, spanning his last two years in the Hanoi Prisoner of War camp, so the token iconic symbol of the American Dream becomes, literally, the butt of the joke.

The language of the monologue is xenophobic bordering on racist; the white clean-cut USAF officer personifies honour, courage and democracy. His references to 'gooks' and 'slopeheads' and 'greasy yella heads' creates tension between the greatest multi-ethnic democracy on earth and the foreign policy it has pursued since the 1930s.

reading the cultural context of pulp fiction

All films must be thoroughly examined in their social, cultural and historical contexts if they are to be properly explained. In making a reading of any film the cultural context should always underpin analysis. There are aspects of contemporary cinema which can be referred to as postmodern, but a number of questions arise if the history of mainstream cinema is not taken into account. These questions are most likely to be posed by those critics who are sceptical of postmodern critical theory.

PULP FICTION AND POPULAR CINEMA

Popular cinema has always been to do with spectacle – this has been the case since the earliest days of silent cinema. However, some commentators on postmodern film seem to assume that spectacle and the mass audience is a new phenomenon. This is clearly disregarding significant aspects of the entire history of film and cinema.

The spectacular blockbusters *Titanic* (1998) and *Star Wars: The Phantom Menace* (1999), to take just two examples, are made very differently from films produced before the 1970s, and this is simply because of what can now be achieved with special effects and digitally generated images. Some would argue that these innovations of spectacle have been at the éxpense of intelligent, coherent narrative, and in the case of some films this may be an acceptable proposition. Nevertheless, taking into account the visual seductiveness of these highly evolved technical advances, it is not to be assumed that one era is less enthralled by spectacle than a previous one, and that narrative-led film is in some way intellectually superior. This said, it is important to be aware that storytelling underpins the bardic function of film and inevitably remains an important attraction to audiences of postmodern films.

historical perspectives

Cinema-going as a ritual of social interaction has changed in many ways since the early twentieth century. Some of these changes have been to do with major events such as world war, but others have been associated with the way we spend our leisure time. During the Depression of the 1930s and the Second World War, cinema provided an escape from the often harsh reality of people's everyday lives, but in the post-war period the escapist experience provided by the movies became a pleasure for its own sake. In the USA the ritual of cinema-going re-shaped itself in the form of the drive-in, wider screens and some short-lived experiments such as 3D and smell-o-vision; and of course, colour had become the norm. From the 1950s cinema suffered a decline in the USA and Britain, in part caused by the spread of television, but the medium was strong enough to persist with its own characteristics alongside and later along with TV.

Cinema in the late twentieth century had been experimenting in many different fields looking for opportunities to recreate the medium. For example, in the late 1980s a bizarre new genre presented itself in the form of *Who Framed Roger Rabbit* (1988) in which the gumshoe detective teamed up with an animated rabbit. Although the film proved to be successful at the box office the experiment went no further. Perhaps the hybrid was an idea that appeared before its time but it has a narrative drive that is equally important to the telling of the stories. Ridley Scott's *Blade Runner* (1982), arguably one of the earliest postmodern classics, could be the latest development in the Frankenstinian genre of man creates complex network of references

man/cyborg film, and it is the power of the connotations of that narrative that is the vehicle of the film's spectacular attributes. As with pre-1970s film, postmodern film is heavily reliant on the appropriate combination and balance of narrative drive and spectacle.

reading pulp fiction as popular culture

Linking our awareness of contemporary society with filmic texts of popular culture is not difficult because both involve mass production and mass consumption. Subject and object have combined to become simulacra and the illusion of anything and everything is apparently possible and available. In this world of frenzied consumption popular culture consumes itself; recycles and recreates itself. This is partly what is going on in *Pulp Fiction* and explains the fractured narrative of the film.

Although the narrative of *Pulp Fiction* is fractured, a complex network of references to popular culture contribute to holding the film together as a coherent whole. At the outset it should be noted that popular culture is more than that which is mass produced, peddled through cynical advertising and marketing campaigns to be bovinely digested by a homogenised mass market of mind-dulled consumers. Neither is it simply the residue that is excluded when judgements are made about what is 'high' culture. Popular culture is a social arena in which individuals, groups and mass formations interact and exchange ideas, attitudes and practices in order to survive and make sense of an increasingly complex and demanding world. Civilisation generates culture, and culture defines itself by the rituals and artefacts it produces. The way we eat, talk, dress and organise our habitat requires a knowledge of rules, rituals, myths and 'realities' that civilisation creates and constantly re-shapes. On a daily basis we negotiate the precarious terrain of the modern world, and popular culture is one of the maps we use on our journey.

Pumpkin and Honey Bunny
plot an assault on one of the
most cherished American
institutions: the diner

the map of popular culture

a microcosm of postmodern america

Pulp Fiction is a kind of 'urban myth' of low life set in an indistinct era somewhere in the city of Los Angeles. Because Tarantino does not use an establishing shot, the diner in the first scene is in no specific place, it is simply any and every diner; a representation of a popular American institution. The audience does not know where it is geographically, but they do know where they are on the map of popular culture. The diner is the site occupied by all types of Americans twenty-four hours a day all over the country. The food is American in all its ethnic manifestations, and the location is off the road or street and specifically there to eat then go. The diner is a different social space to the bar or takeaway, it affords hospitality, sustenance, and a place to rest.

Looking at the diner on screen offers those facilities to the audience vicariously; this venue for popular cultural ritual is used in the opening scene to brutal effect. Pumpkin and Honey Bunny have found a new target for their criminal activity. Pumpkin's accent is English, and Honey Bunny's is unclear but certainly not American, and they are plotting an assault and robbery on one of the most cherished American institutions: the diner. The simple use of the power of popular cultural icons as a vehicle to convey impending terror is the first manipulation of our awareness and understanding of popular culture that Tarantino deploys. In the racial and ethnic melting pot of the US there are no foreigners, only Americans and non-Americans. The hold-up planned is a non-American threat to a wholly American popular-cultural ritual of eating at the diner. The audience is united by this threat.

Later on in the film the Hawthorne Grill metaphorically mutates and becomes Jack Rabbit Slim's; a transformation necessary to create the mise-en-scène in which time is collapsed and the bizarre dinner and dance contest sequence takes place to celebrate 50 years of American popular culture.

postmodern america

Throughout the film the dialogue lapses into a lavish cocktail of ad-speak, pseudo-soap opera lines and TV sit-com clichés. The cautious opening gambits during the dinner date at Jack Rabbit Slim's are made easier when Vincent and Mia take refuge in exchanges using the vocabulary of a variety of popular cultural texts. The b-movie western is referred to as Vincent takes out his tobacco pouch to roll a cigarette:

```
MIA

    Will you roll me one, Cowboy?
VINCENT

    You can have this one, Cowgirl.
```

The forced delivery of the lines gives them the gravity of a much-used quotation from a well-known movie. They go on to discuss Mia's 'fifteen minutes' of fame as Raven McCoy in *Fox Force Five*, a pilot for a TV action adventure show. The format of the show as Mia describes it could be a formula for any one of hundreds of action adventures screened over the past 30 years. The references are piled on and on. When the five-dollar shake arrives the couple go into a sit-com exchange of stilted very-small-talk. Just as Jules had venerated the Kahuna Burger in his humiliation of Brett, in close-up Mia seductively wraps her lips around the drinking straw to take a draught of the shake and pronounces with vivacious approval 'Yummy'. The over-acted parody of ad/sit-com continues until Vincent concurs with Mia's appreciation of the five-dollar shake. His comment bursts the bubble of ad-fantasy within which they acted out the tasting ritual: 'Goddamn! That's a pretty fuckin' good milkshake'. The comic effect of the totally impossible slogan is bathos at its best.

After enduring a short uncomfortable silence Mia teases Vincent about the possibility of their relationship developing, and the date is back in the 'real' world. But the situation very soon drifts back into TV fantasyland as Mia returns from the bathroom, having snorted a line of cocaine with the Steppenwolfish exclamation 'I said Goddamn!' to deliver the excruciatingly trite line 'Don't you just love it when you go to the bathroom and come back to find your food waiting for you'.

The spell of fantasy is interwoven with threads of realism as Vincent demonstrates his knowledge of popular culture by correcting Mia's identification of the look-alikes that wait on the tables. However, they are not referred to as look-alikes when Vincent guarantees that 'that's Marilyn Monroe, and *that's* Mamie Van Doren'. The difference is that Van Doren was only ever a b-movie clone of Marilyn and this pedantic distinction between the two is a clever game engaging the audience's knowledge of the Hollywood star hierarchy. Furthermore, it is heaping up the Hollywood simulacra to raise the challenging question of which, if any, was the real one; and indeed have any of them, from Harlow to Monroe, been anything more than a male fantasy mapped out in film as the ultimate embodiment of the desirable woman.

The crass and exaggerated use of mass-market products and the direct and indirect references to consumerism and popular culture are used to diffuse/create tension and deliberately juxtapose opposites to push product placement and popular cultural clichés ruthlessly to the limits of absurdity. Butch's return to his apartment to collect the gold watch uses an interesting device to enable the shooting of Vincent. Butch's decision to return is a dangerous one. It is likely that there is an ambush waiting for him. Nevertheless, he pursues his hazardous project. The tension in the sequence is built up as he approaches the condo. As Butch stalks the building Tarantino adds one of those deft touches that can pass unnoticed, or provide a piquancy for those with a taste for cleverly cut sequences: just about audible through the open window of another apartment is an advert for Jack Rabbit Slim's, the restaurant where Mia and Vincent had dined and danced on the date. Butch cautiously opens the door to his apartment, the key in the lock shown in a ruthlessly mannered extreme close up, and he takes stock of the situation apprehensively. Having good reason the believe that the coast is clear, his next move is to recover the gold watch. Strangely, rather than immediately taking flight before anything can go wrong, Butch decides to prepare some 'toaster pastries'. This sequence, that sees the end of Vincent, is one of high comedy and violence enriched and enabled by direct reference to popular cultural cliché. As Butch opens the cupboard the visual vernacular of TV advertising prevails; the packet of Sam's Frosted Cinnamon Toaster Pastries is tilted for the brand shot as the camera lingers just long enough in close up for the product to be identified. We then cut to an extreme close up of the pop tarts being put into the toaster. But this time the drift into TV advertisement format is essential to the narrative sequence because it is the pop-up of the cooked toaster pastries that startle Butch into pulling the trigger on Vincent. As a counterpoint to the terrifying rattle of the automatic the smoke alarm bleats with domestic mundanity. Vincent's body is hunched bloodily in the bathtub. He had been reading a cheap edition of *Modesty Blaise* by Peter O'Donnell; a classic example of pulp fiction.

gender representation

The issue of gender representation in *Pulp Fiction* is one that is often glibly dismissed by accepting that Tarantino films are post-feminist as well as postmodern, and women are merely devices used to enhance male qualities, or pornographic dolls onto which voyeuristic male fantasies may be projected. This is not true of the female characters in *Pulp Fiction*. Closer scrutiny reveals a much more involved role for women in the intricate narrative structure. Honey Bunny, Mia Wallace and Esmarelda Villalobos on the surface are crude stereotypes, but they are all portrayed as larger or lower than life according to the comic/violent demands of the narrative. Honey Bunny is a female psychopath parodying female traits as she immerses herself in the male codes of violence. She is a contradiction: as the script notes say 'It is impossible to tell where the young woman is from or how old she is; everything she does contradicts something she did'. As the hold-up goes ahead she knows what she has to do, but has no idea how to do it. Her confused gender representation is a comic/horror histrionic of obscenities. Honey Bunny is a pastiche of the feminine accessories required by the dominant violent male. Girl Friday berserk with a gun.

Mia Wallace appears to pin down Vincent on their first meeting, more so in the director's cut (see Style: Director's Cuts). But her dominance is in the shadow of her menacing new husband, Vincent's boss, Marsellus. Her fate is eventually delivered into the hands of Vincent when he saves her life.

Esmarelda Villalobos is an exotic jungle child, literally barefoot in the urban jungle. In her short exchange with Butch escaping in her taxi she is a sketch of erotic exoticism; her dark Hispanic beauty, her fascination with the dangerous animal Butch, yet totally without a glimmer of fear. Even her name has the lupine connotations of an unfathomable creature of the night.

These thumbnail sketches of a selection of the more central females go some of the way to explain how gender representation works in *Pulp Fiction*, but they do need to be fitted into a broader context. By simply examining gender representations in isolation any analysis will not be as exhaustive as it should be. Comparative analyses have to be made and it must be appreciated that inconclusive grey areas without direct answers can be more significant and fruitful than conclusions that appear black and white.

redemption: a key theme

Redemption is a key theme of *Pulp Fiction*; it is persistently examined and re-examined either implicitly or explicitly in a variety of situations throughout the film. Much criticism and analysis has concentrated on this theme, but it can only be adequately considered if looked at alongside betrayal. All of the characters seeking to redeem themselves need to have something to be forgiven for; betrayal is the act most are guilty of.

In the opening scene Honey Bunny and Pumpkin hatch their plot to hold up the Hawthorne Grill, establishing an incidental enigma that is not resolved until their own redemption, granted by Jules, at the very end of the film.

So from the outset a question is raised about what happens to the two desperate robbers and indeed what should happen to them? In the interim the entire film sets up a series of mises-en-scène that either centrally or peripherally deal with notions of redemption.

As Vincent and Jules go to collect the briefcase from Brett's apartment they discuss the all-powerful position of Marsellus in their lives, and the case of Tony Rocky Horror who, instead of being delivered from his evil act in massaging Mia's feet, was despatched from a fourth-floor window. Instantly the audience identifies Marsellus as someone empowered to pass judgement and dispense justice with absolute impunity. Interestingly, Marsellus remains neither clearly nor fully seen in shot until an hour and a half into the action; he persists as a menacing presence referred to warily by the subservient characters, and functions as an object of macabre curiosity for the audience. Marsellus has a God/Satan like omnipotence poised to mete out either redemption or condemnation using the cruel and unusual codes of mob law.

Under the orders of Marsellus Vincent and Jules are on a mission to collect a briefcase and to avenge the attempted deception of their boss. The requital is conducted with a climactic recitation that ends with the murder of Brett. However, if the text of the tirade is closely examined it is implied that Vincent and Jules are actually on a mission of redemption to despatch Brett for the evil that he has perpetrated on Marsellus. Brett's redemption is death. Brett is condemned as a manifestation of the 'tyranny of evil' whose iniquities include the sin selfishness. Jules assumes that he himself is the shepherd who looks after his brothers, and Brett is one of those who 'attempts to poison and destroy my brothers'. There is no means of escape for Brett; either by way of physical escape from the two hit-men, or escaping the sentence the perverse criminal code prescribes.

Brett's redemption is an ironic redemption; his only salvation is death, and this is later made clear as the range of violent torture that Marsellus is capable of dispensing is unveiled, from the minor punishment inflicted on Tony Rocky Horror to the unthinkable sufferings that Zed is to subjected to when Marsellus assures his rapist that he is 'going medieval' on him. Compared to Zed's fate Brett's death is a merciful relief; he is allowed to die quickly.

redemption: a key theme

professionally and morally culpable

Where Brett's ironic redemption is inescapable death, the next scene sees Butch forced into a professional dilemma by being made an offer he can not refuse. Butch betrays his principles and his natural instincts as a professional boxer. Tarantino measures the pain and suffering of betrayal and redemption not with the precious emotions and feelings of the heroic Hollywood stereotype, but with the washed-out low-lifes that inhabit the vicious hinterland of urban civilisation. Fine feelings and delicate moral struggles are not arenas of emotional conflict exclusive to the sophisticated creations of Woody Allen in his most cloying therapeutic mode; Tarantino permits scum to have feelings too. The fine feelings of allegiance, loyalty, guilt and remorse contemplated and spoken in the language of the streets is a further juxtaposition that discomforts the audience. It wakens the viewer from the comfortable glow of safety and security that normally accompanies the distanced representations of human suffering.

In this case the never-made-it-big professional boxer has to face a crisis of identity and a future without his naturally assumed *raison d'être*. Marsellus makes Butch the offer he can't refuse; he has come to the end of his career because of his age. This scenario is Marsellus's rationalisation of his desire to place a large bet on the fight he has fixed. Butch has as much choice in the 'deal' as Brett had. It seems that Butch is professionally and morally culpable for agreeing to throw the fight, but it becomes apparent that he has a subterfuge that becomes visible later on in the narrative thread. Butch has betrayed his status as a professional fighter by accepting the bribe, but plans to redeem himself of the infringement by double-crossing Marsellus, the architect of his betrayal. Instead of going down in the fifth round of the boxing match as the terms of the bribe required, Butch literally kills his opponent and prepares to collect his own winnings from a series of bets placed on himself to win using Marsellus's bribe money as a stake. This convoluted mise-en-scène of betrayal on betrayal, revenge and redemption forms the basis for a very strange encounter between Butch and the incongruously exotic taxi driver Esmarelda. This is one of the scenes that was heavily cut for the general release of *Pulp Fiction*, but its impact and significance remain.

redemption: a key theme

The taxi cab acts
as a confession box

redemption: a key theme

The taxi cab acts as a confession box. The set is film noir in its most clichéd form; the darkness, passing headlights and spilled neon reflecting from the streets, shot entirely in close-up and extreme close-up. The dialogue is at times barely audible and the sound of the purring engine drifts in and out of the soundtrack.

Butch is in an interesting position for several reasons. Firstly, he does not know that he has killed Floyd Wilson, his opponent in the fixed fight, until Esmarelda tells him what she heard on the radio commentary. Secondly, he has been responsible for the death of a person, but it is a legitimate homicide and not an indictable offence in US criminal law. Thirdly, he has committed an offence under the criminal code by double-crossing Marsellus, an offence that undoubtedly carries a death sentence.

These conditions give rise to some interesting developments in attitudes to loyalty, betrayal and redemption so far. Butch reacts with silent dismay to the realisation that he has killed Floyd Wilson, but he retains the tough fighter's veneer when questioned by Esmarelda. It appears that Butch has had some doubt about his success in perpetuating his lineage as a combat hero; possibly the profession he chose was the closest he could get to emulate the illustrious achievements of his warrior forefathers. Now he has killed a man; a fortuitous event that somehow fulfils his obligation to follow in the family footsteps. Furthermore, he is on the way to a new life in Knoxville with a considerable sum of money and his girlfriend Fabienne. In short, he has redeemed himself of the failure to live up to the reputation of his father, grandfather and great-grandfather.

The irony of killing Wilson legitimately solves one problem of identity for Butch, but irony upon irony occurs through the memory of his revered father. Circumstances betray Butch. Returning to his apartment to collect the iconic wristwatch leads to the encounter with, and murder of, Vincent. Things had looked good until his father's memory in the form of the wristwatch diverted him from escape and back into the vicious world he thought he could leave behind. Although the murder of Vincent redefines Butch as an unlawful killer, it also gives him full spurs as a heroic combatant; maybe not in the field of military confrontation where his ancestors had fought, but for Butch the underworld of Los Angeles is an acceptable theatre of urban warfare.

The double-crossing of Marsellus leads to one of the most dramatic narrative threads to be resolved by redemption. The encounter with Marsellus at the interchange stretches coincidence to its limits, and the meeting is both comic and ironic. The last thing that could go wrong has done: Butch meets his judge, jury and executioner en route to his flight and salvation. The next curious turn of events occurs in the basement dungeon of Maynard's shop. Butch makes his escape as Marsellus is being raped by Zed, and kills a third victim, The Gimp, in the process. It is difficult to speculate what makes Butch decide not to leave Marsellus at the mercy of Zed and Maynard. Marsellus had put a contract out on Butch because of his betrayal, and there is no doubt that Butch would have assumed this; Vincent and Marsellus had been waiting to ambush him should he be rash enough to return to his apartment. Could it have been some kind of loyalty among men that no man should suffer the sexual assault and degradation that Marsellus was undergoing? Whatever the motivation was, Butch risked all in deciding to forgive Marsellus for trying to kill him, and going back to rescue him. Butch approaches the redemption with ritual gravity, choosing the Samurai sword as a sacrificial token; he knows he will have to kill again in order to release Marsellus. Having killed Maynard, his fourth victim, and taken control of the situation, Butch waits for the decision of Marsellus on 'what happens next'. Marsellus in turn forgives Butch. He may have done this for a combination of reasons. First, because he was indebted to Butch for saving him from the probably fatal appetites of Zed and Maynard. And second, because even the omnipotent Marsellus's reputation would not be able to recover from the humiliation of rape by a hillbilly white boy. So the agreement is made that Butch will be spared and free to go so long as he never comes back to tell of what went on in the partition of the basement ominously referred to as 'Russell's old room'.

Redemption closes the narrative threads too. At the end of the film the hold-up of the Hawthorne Grill gets underway. Honey Bunny and Pumpkin seem to be doing well in the robbery until they are confronted by a diner less terrified by their threats and shrieked orders to give up cash and valuables. Jules stands his ground with the mysterious briefcase, and amid Pumpkin's amazement at the glimpse of the contents Jules is able to draw his own gun. During the stand-off that follows Jules and Vincent gain the upper hand in both confidence and capability. They could kill Honey Bunny and Pumpkin, taking or leaving the spoils of the robbery, but in a bizarre act of forgiveness Jules persuades the robbers that it is in their best interest to take what they have got along with $1500 of his own money thrown in.

So where the movie starts in narrative context it also ends; and the most powerful leitmotif in the text, the relationship between loyalty, betrayal and redemption, brackets the film by way of prologue and epilogue.

violence and humour: a key theme

Much has been said about the violence in Tarantino films in general, and *Pulp Fiction* in particular (see The Critics), but the fact is that a closer examination of the film shows that there is only a relatively small amount of physical violence at all. Furthermore, there is even less actually visible to the audience. Throughout the film violence is used as a vehicle for humour, and the humour is deliberately conflated with violence. There is the smouldering insinuation of menace that is passed from scene to scene, and from character to character. At precisely calculated junctures in the text that menacing presence erupts into either implied physical violence, portrayals of actual physical violence, or a much more profound and discomforting non-physical humiliation. Where Tarantino lost control of some of the violent scenes in the 'experimental' *Reservoir Dogs*, in *Pulp Fiction* he exploited a much more successful device to convey manifestations of vehement ill-will and harm. He laid down the usual filmic abbreviations around which the audience uses their perception and imagination to build up their reading of the narrative. But then comes the uncomfortable realisation that the learned method of reading

'Now you got a corpse
in a car, minus a head,
in a garage.'

an essay in psychopathy

classic Hollywood narrative has not come up with the usual pay-off. The audience is given no safe option of reaction other than to laugh at what is not normally within the bounds of comedy. The first incidence of this effect is during the collection of the briefcase at Brett's apartment. The physical violence is limited to Roger being killed with a single shot, and Brett is wounded before being murdered out of shot with a salvo of gunfire.

Violence is an important feature of the gangster/thriller, but as with all the other clichés wrought into the text it too is parodied. Tarantino is both playing the game and at the same time breaking the rules by questioning the codes of the genre. Vincent and Jules step into character and enter the apartment with the professional detachment demanded by audience expectation, the mise-en-scène and by the unfolding of the narrative so far. Immediately they set about their tasks; Vincent melts ominously into the background of the scene, a straight man for Jules's ranting diatribe, where he lurks vigilantly. Jules begins his systematic humiliation of Brett. The dialogue is an essay in psychopathy, introducing more of the leitmotifs that persist throughout the film; popular culture, consumerism and pastiche.

The threat of humour is buried deeply in the scene and emerges sporadically during the verbal lashing inflicted upon Brett. For example, Jules picks up again his ruminations on the generics of the American burger, to the amazement of Brett, and for the amusement of Vincent and the audience. The boys are terrified by the eloquence of the language and the dangerously simmering alternation between affability and arrogance displayed by their interrogator. Jules assaults Brett's personal territory by taking his Kahuna Burger and performing his sampling of it using the mundane language of advertising. The camera cuts to an extreme close-up of the burger taken directly from the visual vernacular of TV commercials, and Jules lapses into a string of declarations that are indistinguishable from ad slogans: 'Hamburgers: the cornerstone of any nutritious breakfast'; 'Ummmm, that's a tasty burger'; 'Well, if you like hamburgers give 'em a try sometime', and of the Sprite drink 'Ummmm, hits the spot!'.

violence and humour

Tension is deceptively relaxed when Vincent locates the briefcase he and Jules had come to collect. Brett miscalculates the gangsters' game plan by assuming that now the 'object of desire', the briefcase, has been recovered the heat is off. Courting danger, Brett tries to reason with Jules and seeks redemption. Jules continues to drift erratically between the affability of ad-speak and the menace of thinly veiled insults and threats. He builds himself up to the casual murder of Roger, the 'flock of seagulls' boy fear-frozen in recline on a sofa. This shooting is the first instance of extreme violence set in a comedic context. The power and content of the dialogue, and the narrative sequence, have built up the nervous expectation of the audience and they respond, through cathexis, by laughing at the nonchalant murder of Roger. In a cinema auditorium of first-time viewers this response is often rapidly followed by an atmosphere of collective discomfort, as people realise that they have found the portrayal of indifferent, cold-blooded murder amusing.

Brett now knows for sure his fate will be the same as Roger's, and Jules is aware of this. The teasing of a weaker and defenceless victim who is aware that he is in the hands of a psychopathic killer and soon to die is a similar situation to the ear-cutting scene in *Reservoir Dogs*. However, Tarantino deploys humour and the device of bizarre parody. Having murdered Roger in a casual gesture of the gun, Jules continues his interrogation and the dialogue becomes a vaudevillian exchange rocking playfully on the fulcrum of Brett's repeated terrified response with the word 'what' to Jules's questions. Again the humour is juxtaposed with sudden violence as Jules shoots Brett in the shoulder. The audience is on a macabre rollercoaster and running out of legitimate options for engagement with the text. At this point Tarantino throws out a line, and the audience is relieved by being given the opportunity to react with surprise at Jules's switch from heaping obscenity upon obscenity to posing the simple and incongruous question to Brett: 'You ever read the Bible?'

Jules then goes into a long ranting speech, incorrectly credited as coming from Ezekiel 25:17. The misquoted parody is more biblical than the real thing. Tarantino has scripted a fire and brimstone rationale of why Brett

a deliberate overkill

has to pay for his betrayal of Marsellus with his life. The speech is a statement of the perverse logic of honour among thieves. The comic aspect of the monologue is that it is spoken with a tone and delivery that assures us that Jules knows that he is right in what he is about to do. He is about to engage in the work of God. There is no redemption for those who break the ultimate rules, and Jules is justified in carrying out the execution as a 'righteous man'. This is the drug dealer and murderer who is speaking and the incongruity of that is comically absurd. The volley of gunfire that kills Brett is a point of view shot that puts the audience in the position of the victim. The sound is exaggerated and the volley of shots is, literally, a deliberate overkill.

A similar device juxtaposing humour and dramatic overkill is the accidental killing of Marvin. In the reconstructed narrative this happens after Vincent, Jules and Marvin have left the scene of Roger and Brett's murder. The fractured narrative is taken up with an overlap of the action in the apartment. A fourth young man had been hiding and after Brett is killed the fourth young man tries to shoot his way out by taking Vincent and Jules by surprise. They survive the hail of bullets fired at point-blank range in the unsuccessful ambush. Jules is convinced that their survival was due to divine intervention, and it was a signal from God that he had been spared, and he must give up 'the life' working for Marsellus. This realisation by Jules that he has been chosen by God has a cutting irony, emphasised by his chiding of Vincent for blaspheming; and the masterstroke is delivered as Vincent accidentally shoots Marvin in the face: 'Why the fuck did you do that?' asks Jules. Again the audience is trapped into laughing at the death of a young man.

the critics

Pulp Fiction won the Palme d'Or for best film at the 1994 Cannes Film Festival, The Golden Globe Award for Best Screenplay; Best Picture, Los Angeles Film Critics Awards; and Best Screenplay, New York Film Critics Circle Awards.

One of the most informed critical reviews was by Alan A. Stone:

the critics

If you take no pleasure in popular culture, with all its manic excesses, then you are likely to be bewildered, even offended, by Quentin Tarantino's extraordinary film, Pulp Fiction. Tarantino unapologetically enjoys popular culture at the same time that he satirises it. Unfortunately, he also seems to specialise in violence. Still, taken on its own terms, Pulp Fiction is a rare accomplishment; it opens a new aesthetic horizon in film. Like Van Gogh's sunflowers, the ordinary suddenly takes on a striking vibrancy; from the dazzling title colors on, it is easy to recognise the artist, but almost impossible to imagine how one could imitate him. Tarantino, a one-time video store clerk, now the hottest director in Hollywood, has memory banks packed with movies and he draws on some of the most ordinary to create something brilliantly original. This is no experimental film of intellectual pretensions and highbrow obscurantism. Pulp Fiction is already building a cult following, even as its mother-fucker language and graphic violence offends others.

Violence in film is a serious matter, and for some people an inexcusable offence. They can see no justification for the scene in which John Travolta's character accidentally blows a young man's brains out. Even worse for those concerned about film violence, most of the audience laughed despite the spatter of blood and brain tissue; and with spontaneous amusement, not the nervous hysteria often heard at horror films. The violence of Pulp Fiction is essential to its aesthetic; though he knew that many would complain, Tarantino meant the audience to laugh. Deliberately violating the conventions of action-violence films, Tarantino reimagines stylised moments of violence and exaggerates them until they are almost surrealistic.

Alan A. Stone, The Boston Review, 1994

This extract from Stone's critique is one of the best informed and equable write-ups considering the vast rash of commentary that broke out following the general release of *Pulp Fiction* in the USA on 14 October 1994. It is worth noting here that when *Pulp Fiction* was released outside the United States a couple of weeks later the European critics would already have seen screenings some time before the general release in their own countries, but, broadly speaking, they would have taken their lead from their American counterparts.

Stone, in his lengthy review, seems to need to slot *Pulp Fiction* into a category in the standard Hollywood taxonomy, and going further, into the altogether wider continuum that divides high culture and low/popular culture. His confusion is probably due to *Pulp Fiction* having the 'art-house' movie look, yet its entire underpinning and subject matter is peppered with the mass-produced pulp artefacts of popular culture. *Pulp Fiction* is not the first motion picture to do this, but where it differs is that it is a celebration of what has been routinely ridiculed and devalued as the low practices, products and rituals of a popular culture given its place in the natural order of things somewhere (anywhere) below what is deemed to be high culture.

From the outset of the article Stone makes his culturalist credentials clear by implying that popular culture can only be measured by the indices of taste and judgement laid down by those who are appointed as the keepers of culture; and those keepers cosily reside in the castle above, while the mass audiences of popular culture stand waiting at the gate.

Stone suggests that *Pulp Fiction* should be 'taken on its own terms'. This is a recommendation that usually protects the critic from addressing issues that threaten to subvert his own position. The very questions that rattle the shingles of the ivory towers under which culturalist aestheticism reproduces and perpetuates itself and its values.

Using the vocabulary and vernacular of cultural elitism, Stone can only attempt to appropriate *Pulp Fiction* into some corner of his aesthetic territory to cleanse it of any oppositional or subversive tendency. This is a tried and tested process; the self-protect mode of culturalism that insulates it from challenge by sceptics. The Tarantino problem, making films that ask difficult questions about traditional aesthetic judgement while at the same time make millions of dollars for Hollywood, has to be solved.

'the glib violence'

There are many interesting and informative reviews and critiques available in archives, for example Leah Welborn records some thought-provoking quotations from a question and answer session with Tarantino:

> After the film, the audience was allowed to ask questions of Tarantino and co-host Richard Linklater. In response to a question concerning the glib violence that serves as a backbone for his work, Tarantino said, 'What I'm trying to do more than anything else is, I like the idea of making things funny that you've never seen be funny. I like to break it down to the banal. You take genre characters and you put them in a situation, and they don't react just like genre characters in a movie.'
>
> *The Daily Texan, October 1994*

Furthermore, there are shorter accounts and opinions that can be used as a vehicle to mobilise debate about *Pulp Fiction*. Rob Marcato writing in *The Tech* observes that

> In a film whose praise has been mostly due to its originality, these tales of hit men and criminals are certainly nothing we haven't seen before. So, what is it that makes the film so fresh and so unlike anything before it? The key does not lie in Pulp Fiction's plot-line but, instead, in its writer and director, Quentin Tarantino.
>
> *The Tech, October 1994, volume 114, number 49*

bibliography

general film

Altman, Rick, *Film Genre*,
BFI, 1999
    Detailed exploration of film genres

Bordwell, David, *Narration in the Fiction Film*, Routledge, 1985
    A detailed study of narrative theory and structures

– – –, Staiger, Janet & Thompson, Kristin, *The Classical Hollywood Cinema: Film Style & Mode of Production to 1960*, Routledge, 1985; pbk 1995
    An authoritative study of cinema as institution, it covers film style and production

– – – & Thompson, Kristin, *Film Art*, McGraw-Hill, 4th edn, 1993
    An introduction to film aesthetics for the non-specialist

Branson, Gill & Stafford, Roy, *The Media Studies Handbook*, Routledge, 1996

Buckland, Warren, *Teach Yourself Film Studies*, Hodder & Stoughton, 1998
    Very accessible, it gives an overview of key areas in film studies

Cook, Pam (ed.), *The Cinema Book*, BFI, 1994

Corrigan, Tim, *A Short Guide To Writing About Film*,
HarperCollins, 1994
    What it says: a practical guide for students

Dyer, Richard, *Stars*, BFI, 1979; pbk Indiana University Press, 1998
    A good introduction to the star system

Easthope, Antony, *Classical Film Theory*, Longman, 1993
    A clear overview of recent writing about film theory

Hayward, Susan, *Key Concepts in Cinema Studies*,
Routledge, 1996

Hill, John & Gibson, Pamela Church (eds), *The Oxford Guide to Film Studies*, Oxford University Press, 1998
    Wide-ranging standard guide

Lapsley, Robert & Westlake, Michael, *Film Theory: An Introduction*,
Manchester University Press, 1994

Maltby, Richard & Craven, Ian, *Hollywood Cinema*,
Blackwell, 1995
    A comprehensive work on the Hollywood industry and its products

Mulvey, Laura, 'Visual Pleasure and Narrative Cinema' (1974), in Visual and Other Pleasures,
Indiana University Press, Bloomington, 1989
    The classic analysis of 'the look' and 'the male gaze' in Hollywood cinema. Also available in numerous other edited collections

Nelmes, Jill (ed.), *Introduction to Film Studies*,
Routledge, 1996
    Deals with several national cinemas and key concepts in film study

Nowell-Smith, Geoffrey (ed.), *The Oxford History of World Cinema*,
Oxford University Press, 1996
    Hugely detailed and wide-ranging with many features on 'stars'

Thomson, David, *A Biographical Dictionary of the Cinema*, Secker & Warburg, 1975
  Unashamedly driven by personal taste, but often stimulating

Truffaut, François, *Hitchcock*, Simon & Schuster, 1966, rev. edn, Touchstone, 1985
  Landmark extended interview

Turner, Graeme, *Film as Social Practice*, 2nd edn, Routledge, 1993
  Chapter four, 'Film Narrative', discusses structuralist theories of narrative

Wollen, Peter, *Signs and Meaning in the Cinema*, Viking, 1972
  An important study in semiology

Readers should also explore the many relevant websites and journals. *Film Education* and *Sight and Sound* are standard reading.

Valuable websites include:

The Internet Movie Database at http://uk.imdb.com

Screensite at http://www.tcf.ua.edu/screensite/contents.html

The Media and Communications Site at the University of Aberystwyth at http://www.aber.ac.uk/~dgc/welcome.html

There are obviously many other university and studio websites which are worth exploring in relation to film studies.

pulp fiction

Balio, T. (ed.), *Hollywood in the Age of Television*, Unwin Hyman, 1990

Belton, John, *American Cinema/ American Culture*, McGraw Hill, 1994

Falcon, R., *Classified! A Teacher's Guide to Film and Video Censorship and Classification*, BFI, 1994

Fiske, John, *Introduction to Communication Studies*, 2nd edn, Routledge, 1990

Rosenberg, B. and White, D. (eds), *Mass Culture*, Free Press, 1957

Ross, A., *No Respect: Intellectuals and Popular Culture*, Routledge, 1989

Ross Muir, A., 'The status of women working in film and television', in L. Gamman & M. Marshment (eds), *The Female Gaze: Women as Viewers of Popular Culture*, The Women's Press, London, 1988

Rylance, R., *Roland Barthes*, Harvester Wheatsheaf, 1994

Storey, J., *An Introductory Guide to Cultural Theory and Popular Culture*, Harvester Wheatsheaf, 1993

Strinati, D. and Wagg, S. (eds), *Come on Down?: Popular Media Culture in Post-war Britain*, Routledge, 1992

reviews and articles

Donald & Scanlan, 'Hollywood Feminism? Get Real', *Trouble & Strife*, Vol. 2, Winter 1992

'Pulp Fiction',
The Christian Science Monitor,
14 September 1995

'Tarantino the Icon Captures Britain',
Los Angeles Times,
4 February 1995

'Pulp Fiction',
The Wall Street Journal,
10 January 1995

'Pulp Fiction: Top Award from
National Film Critics',
The New York Times, 4 January 1995

'Pulp Fiction',
The New York Times, January 1995

'Pulp Fiction',
The New York Review of Books,
6 April 1995

'Quentin Tarantino', *Newsweek,*
26 December 1994

'An Auteur is Born', *Premiere,*
November 1994

'Pulp Fiction', *America,*
12 November 1994

'On The News', *Insight,*
7 November 1994

'Pulp Fiction', *Harper's Bazaar,*
October 1994

'Pulp Fiction', *Los Angeles Magazine,*
October 1994

'Pulp Fiction', *Vogue,*
October 1994

'Pulp Fiction', *Time,*
October 1994

cinematic terms

accelerated montage a sequence made up of shots of increasingly shorter lengths that creates a psychological atmosphere of excitement and tension

aerial shot a shot from above, usually made from plane, helicopter, or crane

asynchronous sound sound that does not proceed directly from the film image

auteur a director with a recognisable and distinctive style who is considered the prime 'author' of a film

back light lighting directed at the camera from behind the subject, thus silhouetting the subject. See key light

boom the mobile arm that suspends the microphone above the actors and outside of the frame

Brechtian referring to the theories of film and theatre held by Marxist poet and playwright Bertolt Brecht. Challenges the audience's conventional suspension of disbelief

cahiers du cinéma Paris-based film journal founded by André Bazin and Jacques Doniol-Valcroze in 1951 that featured important articles by future directors of the French New Wave

camera angle the perspective that the camera takes on the subject that is being shot. low angle, high angle, or tilt angle are the three most commonly used

cathexis collective response of an audience

chiaroscuro the artistic technique of arranging light and dark elements in pictorial composition

cinematography motion-picture photography

cinéma vérité literally, 'cinema truth'. Derived from the work of Jean Rouch the term describes a particular kind of cinema that uses easily adaptable equipment, small crews, and direct interviews. . The Blair Witch Project (1999) is probably the most recent and extreme example of hyper-cinéma vérité to achieve mainstream box-office success

close-up in its precise meaning, a shot of the subject's face or other object alone; more generally, any close shot

compilation film a film whose shots, clips etc and sequences come from other films, often archive or newsreel footage

continuity editing editing shots together apparently seamlessly, so that the action of a sequence appears to be continuous

crane shot a shot taken from a camera mounted on a dolly with a boom that moves up and down. To 'crane' is to move the camera up or down

crosscutting intercutting shots from two or more sequences, clips, or stories to imply parallel action

cultural capital the level of education, social experience, class, social standing and cultural awareness that an individual is able to bring to a text, to enable them to understand and appreciate it. Cultural capital is notion extensively explored by French critic Pierre Bourdieu

cutting (cut to) moving from one image or shot to another by editing

cinematic terms

establishing shot a shot, usually a long shot, that positions the audience in a film narrative by providing visual information (such as location) for the scene that follows

extreme long shot a shot made from a considerable distance, sometimes as far as a quarter of a mile. It provides a panoramic view of a location without camera movement

fade-in a technique for beginning a scene whereby an image gradually appears on a blackened screen, finally brightening into full visibility

fade-out the opposite technique to fade-in

film noir a French term (literally, 'black film') for a film set in a gritty urban atmosphere that deals with profound passions and violent crime. The late forties saw many thrillers made in this genre

final cut a film in its completed form

flashback a shot, scene, sequence, inserted into the narrative present in order to refer the narrative past

flash forward like a flashback, a shot, scene; or sequence outside the narrative present, but referring the narrative future

fractured narrative linear narrative deliberately broken up and reconstituted to challenge convention

frame the smallest compositional unit of film structure, the frame is the individual photographic image on the filmstrip. Framing also designates the boundaries of the image

freeze frame a shot that replicates a still photograph

full shot a shot that shows the subject's entire body and often a three-quarters view of the set

hand-held a type of shot made from the shoulder or by holding the camera in the hand

intertextuality the function of separate texts operating by referring to each other, e.g. TV advertising borrowing images from movies

jouissance (see also *plaisir*) a term used by the French semiologist Roland Barthes. A word difficult to translate into English but describes the thrill of pleasure. *Jouissance* destabilises the comfortable condition of *plaisir* and gives a more uncomfortable, disruptive and threatening thrill

jump cut a cut that is made in the middle of a continuous shot, or a mismatched cut between shots. Jump cuts are used create discontinuity in film time and space

key light main light source on a film set

key to the narrative a term referring to 'he who holds the key to the narrative.' Usually a single character, usually a male, whose actions in the narrative determine its outcomes and resolution

kickers sometimes called 'eye' lights, they are filler lights that supplement the key lights

long shot a shot that includes the whole figures of its subjects and a lot of background

make strange (*verfremdung*) a Brechtian notion referring to a deliberate effort to draw attention to

cinematic terms

the fact that a piece of drama is only a construction, by making it feel strange to the audience

Marxist Marxist theory suggests that those who own the means of production have control in capitalist societies. In the context of film it can be argued that mainstream narrative cinema reinforces the capitalist system by reproducing its dominant ideologies

match cut a cut in which two different shots are linked by soundtrack or visual continuity

medium shot a shot distanced midway between a close-up and a full shot

mise-en-scène literally, 'putting in the scene'. A term that describes the props, action, lighting, décor and so on in the shot itself. In a more closely analytical context mise-en-scène can refer to the way particular conditions are created within which the narrative can unfold

narrative film a film whose structure follows a storyline of some sort. The mainstream of film history from the medium's birth through the present has been narrative

off-screen space the implied space beyond the borders of the film frame at any given moment in projection

pan a pivotal movement of the camera around a vertical axis. Normally no more than 180

plaisir (see also *jouissance*) a term used by the French semiologist Roland Barthes. A word difficult to translate into English but is sometimes interpreted as 'pleasure' in a comfortable, reassuring and soothing sense. *Plaisir* is complacent and compatible with the tradition of a

conventionally safe and comfortable reading of a film

postmodernism a problematic term used to describe many aspects of contemporary cultural production and experience including architecture, art, music, digital media, film and television. One of postmodernism's key characteristics is its eclecticism; it borrows from earlier as well as contemporary styles to produce new aesthetic combinations and cultural formations. Postmodernism also plays with and manipulates paradigms intertextually

Propp Vladimir Propp isolated the narrative pattern of 100 Russian folk tales in the 1920s. His theories are part of Russian Formalism

proxemics the distance between people

realism the term realism is one of the most problematic in the field of Film Studies. Realism can mean 'true to life', or it can refer to a realist effect that is created by unrealistic devices. For example, an extreme close up shot may be used to increase tension in realist film, yet most extreme close-ups are a point of view rarely seen in ordinary human experience. The discussion and analysis of Realism can only go on to be more problematic as progress is made in new digital technologies

real time the actual time it would take for an event to occur in reality, outside of a film

rushes the sound and images of each session's shooting, rapidly processed, so that the decision makers can evaluate what has been done so far before shooting begins again

cinematic terms

score the musical soundtrack for a film

simulacra deceptive image of something that's been reproduced over and over again

subjective camera a technique that causes the viewer to observe events from the perspective of a character in the film (also point of view)

Todorov Tzvetan Todorov was born in Bulgaria and contributed to the Russian Formalist school of criticism. He developed a narrative theory based on a pattern of cause and effect

tracking shot a continuous shot made with a moving camera mounted on a dolly

voice-over a voice track laid over the film's sound mix to narrate, describe or comment on the action on screen

wide-angle lens a lens whose broad angle of view increases the illusion of depth

zoom a variable-focus lens often used to create optical motion without tracking the camera

credits

producers
Lawrence Bender
Danny DeVito

executive producers
Richard N. Gladstein
Stacey Sher
Bob Weinstein

co-executive producers
Michael Shamberg (I)
Harvey Weinstein

cinematography
Andrzej Sekula

film editing
Sally Menke

casting
Ronnie Yeskel and Gary M. Zuckerbrod

production design
David Wasco

art direction
Charles Collum

set decoration
Sandy Reynolds-Wasco

costume design
Betsy Heimann

assistant hair stylist, assistant makeup artist
Christina Bartolucci

makeup effects (as Tom Bellissimo)
Thomas L. Bellissimo

special makeup supervisors
Howard Berger and Gregory Nicotero

key makeup artist
Michelle Bühler

wig maker
Bill Fletcher (II)

key hair stylist
Audree Futterman

production manager
Paul Hellerman

cast
Tim Roth – Pumpkin
Amanda Plummer – Honey Bunny
Laura Lovelace – Waitress
John Travolta – Vincent Vega
Samuel L. Jackson – Jules Winnfield
Phil LaMarr – Marvin
Frank Whaley – Brett
Burr Steers – Roger
Bruce Willis – Butch Coolidge
Ving Rhames – Marsellus Wallace
Paul Calderon – Paul
Bronagh Gallagher – Trudy

credits

Rosanna Arquette – Jody

Eric Stoltz – Lance

Uma Thurman – Mia

Jerome Patrick Hoban –
Ed Sullivan look alike

Michael Gilden –
Phillip Morris Page

Gary Shorelle –
Ricky Nelson look alike

Susan Griffiths –
Marilyn Monroe look alike

Eric Clark – James Dean look alike

Josef Pilato –
Dean Martin look alike

Brad Parker – Jerry Lewis look alike

Steve Buscemi –
Buddy Holly look alike

Lorelei Leslie –
Mamie Van Doren look alike

Emil Sitka –
'Hold hands, you love birds!'

Brenda Hillhouse – Butch's Mother

Christopher Walken –
Captain Koons

Chandler Lindauer – Young Butch

Sy Sher – Klondike

Robert Ruth – Sportscaster One

Rich Turner – Sportscaster Two

Angela Jones –
Esmarelda Villalobos

Don Blakely – Wilson's Trainer

Carl Allen – Dead Floyd Wilson

Maria de Medeiros – Fabienne

Karen Maruyama – Gawker

Kathy Griffin – Herself

Venessia Valentino – Pedestrian

Linda Kaye – Shot Woman

Duane Whitaker – Maynard

Peter Greene – Zed

Stephen Hibbert – The Gimp

Alexis Arquette – Fourth Man

Quentin Tarantino – Jimmie

Venessia Valentino – Bonnie

Harvey Keitel – Winston Wolf

Julia Sweeney – Raquel

Lawrence Bender –
Long Hair Yuppie Scum

Dick Miller – Monster Joe

Other titles in the series

Other titles available in the York Film Notes series:

Title	ISBN
8½ (Otto e mezzo)	0582 40488 6
A bout de souffle	0582 43182 4
Apocalypse Now	0582 43183 2
Battleship Potemkin	0582 40490 8
Blade Runner	0582 43198 0
Casablanca	0582 43200 6
Chinatown	0582 43199 9
Citizen Kane	0582 40493 2
Das Cabinet des Dr Caligari	0582 40494 0
Double Indemnity	0582 43196 4
Dracula	0582 43197 2
Easy Rider	0582 43195 6
Fargo	0582 43193 X
Fear Eats the Soul	0582 43224 3
La Haine	0582 43194 8
Lawrence of Arabia	0582 43192 1
Psycho	0582 43191 3
Romeo and Juliet	0582 43189 1
Some Like It Hot	0582 40503 3
Stagecoach	0582 43187 5
Taxi Driver	0582 40506 8
The Full Monty	0582 43181 6
The Godfather	0582 43188 3
The Piano	0582 43190 5
The Searchers	0582 40510 6
The Terminator	0582 43186 7
The Third Man	0582 40511 4
Thelma and Louise	0582 43184 0
Unforgiven	0582 43185 9

Also from York Notes

Also available in the **York Notes** range:

York Notes
The ultimate literature guides for GCSE students (or equivalent levels)

York Notes Advanced
Literature guides for A-level and undergraduate students (or equivalent levels)

York Personal Tutors
Personal tutoring on essential GCSE English and Maths topics

Available from good bookshops.
For full details, please visit our website at www.longman-yorknotes.com

PULP FICTION

notes

notes